Promo Paks
Nearly-Free Marketing
for Authors

(New and Improved)

Promo Paks
Nearly-Free Marketing for Authors

(New and Improved)

By

Janet Elaine Smith

A Star Publish LLC Book
http://starpublish.com

*Promo Paks: Nearly-Free Marketing for Authors
(New and Improved)*
©Janet Elaine Smith 2007

ISBN: 1-932993-87-8
ISBN 13: 978-1-932993-87-5

Library of Congress Number
LCCN: 2007942188

Edited by Star Publish LLC
Cover Design by Star Publish LLC
Interior Design by Mystique Design

Published in 2007 by Star Publish LLC
Printed in the United States of America

Contents

A great way to keep the mundane interviews from bogging down by doing an informal "live" interview.

How to get them in all over the country by "customizing" your book to different geographical areas. Also includes a detailed up-to-date list of links to two major newspapers in each of the 50 states.

How to write and sell your family secrets without making enemies. Gives detailed instructions on what to include when you write your family history as well as several libraries which specialize in genealogical collections. Also several genealogy magazines that are ripe markets in an ever-expanding field.

How to build your credits in this market, as well as how to make the leap from the small, non-paying periodicals to popular periodicals like Guideposts. Includes a list of some of the magazines, as well as many fictional book publishers in this hot niche. Even Harlequin is getting into the inspirational romance field!

Showing the writers how to gear their books at specific times of the year so they have a better chance of getting book sales. Includes a list of several "popular" books that fit this scenario so they can study what works.

Provides a sample script, as well as instructions on how to steer the interviewer where you want him to go.

How to create your own e-group and how to keep it active. Also includes a good list of many active writers e-groups that will not only provide good sales possibilities (yes, good writers are good readers), but good moral support as well.

How to make the best use of them. Tricks that will get you listed without much effort. Provides a list of numerous search engines.

How to share what you know by teaching classes through the public libraries, adult education, writers groups, etc. Gives a sample curriculum for a six-week course.

How to make your newsletter work for you. Includes how to get your information included in other authors' newsletters.

A walk-through with suggestions of what to include. Includes a walk through Janet Elaine Smith's web site and why she has what she has.

How to get your books listed in thousands of online and brick and mortar bookstores without leaving home. Includes an online experiment that put Janet Elaine Smith's books in well over 1000 online bookstores.

How and where to get them and how to make them a success. Suggestions for the "unusual" that will bring people running—even if they don't like what you write. Includes how to set up a "group signing" even if you don't know any other authors. Also in this segment is information on contests.

How to get them scheduled and how to keep them from falling asleep.

How to beat them at their own game and get POD books into them all across the country. Shows how to utilize the "friends and neighbors" philosophy to accomplish what the "big boys" claim is impossible.

What to do so your book is known everywhere you go, without seeming obnoxious. Places to flaunt it, how to's on getting it recognized around the country. Useful phone tactics, etc. Lots of good examples in this one.

How to travel from blog to blog without ever leaving home.

Riding on the "big players'" shirttails.

Chapter 1
MY DREAM: TO BE ON THE SHELVES

Every author dreams of walking into a bookstore, going over to the shelf, picking their own book out and standing there admiring it. It is probably the "ultimate goal" for every author. Can't you see your name there beside John Grisham, Stephen King, Mary Higgins Clark or Nora Roberts?

Then, unfortunately, reality sets in. Not only has your book not been sent by case lots to every bookstore in the country, the big chain bookstore in your own town looks at you with a question mark when you ask them to put a dozen or so copies on their shelves.

So where do you go from there? Is it hopeless? If so, should you just accept the fact that a few family members and close friends will buy your book, and it will be lost to the rest of the world? Or do you take the bull by the horns and try to find a solution to your dilemma?

For those of you who are brave enough to try to buck the system and pursue your dream, these are some practical tips on how to break the barriers and get your books out where people will actually see them—and buy them. Yes, you *can* get them into the stores like Barnes & Noble, but it isn't easy.

This portion of the book comes with a warning: *This is not for cowards. If you are going to succeed, you have to employ some "tough love." You won't like some of what I say, but you agreed to jump on the merry-go-round. You can jump off any time you want to, but don't slow it down too much for the rest of the authors who want to ride it until they have their full dollar's worth.*

Chapter 2
WHERE TO BEGIN

I have found that some of the most basic business principles are found in the Bible. You don't have to be of any particular religious persuasion to recognize that many a college English professor has cited the Bible as one of the most perfect examples of English literature. So put your prejudices aside for a minute and consider this.

In Acts 1:8 it says, "and ye shall be witnesses unto me both in Jerusalem, and in all Judaea, and in Samaria, and unto the uttermost part of the earth."

Jerusalem signifies your own back yard. This is the best place to start. If you already have a book published, hopefully you will have begun this aspect of your marketing efforts. It is vital that you get acquainted with the manager and the clerks at your local stores. For this section, we are concentrating on the big chains (i.e. the uttermost part of the earth), and this is true there. If you want their business, you should have been giving them yours for months, if not years, before you ever had a book of your own available.

Assuming you have already done that, take your book and head for the Barnes & Noble, Hastings, Borders or whatever is in your town. Show them your book proudly, then ask them if they would order a few copies. It is at this point that you will be tempted to go into "defense mode." Why? Because there are many things that come into play here. Remember, these people are there primarily to make money. There were nearly 300,000 new books published in 2006, and that is constantly growing. Shelf space is at a premium. The big New York publishers are actually paying big bucks to get the prime display areas in the stores.

I will give you some of the most common arguments bookstore managers offer—on a daily basis. However, I will also offer some good "arguments," which should never be "argued," but you should use your traits of gentle persuasion and powerful debate to get your point across.

Many of these issues have prerequisites. We will address them as we come to each point. If you have not already done those things, go back and do them, then come back to the bookstore, proof in hand that their arguments are not relevant.

Where can we order your book? This is one of those things that you should have considered when you went shopping for a publisher/ independent book supplier/print-on-demand company. It is absolutely imperative that your publisher has a good distribution program in place. At the very least, their books should be available through Ingram and Baker & Taylor. Assuming that it is, your reply is quite simple.

"It is available through Ingram. Here is the ISBN to make it easier for you to look up." (Hand them your book, with the number readily available, at this point.)

As they punch your numbers into the computer, it is not out of line to make some small talk about your book. Well ahead of approaching them, practice a one or two line "pitch" for your book. You worked hard to get a "hook" for the first line in your book when you were writing it; it is equally as important to have that "hook" for your marketing efforts. The following is an example:

"Children are being stolen right and left these days. *Stolen in the Storm* is a frightening story of a travel nurse who was accused of stealing some of those babies." (Refers to a romantic intrigue written by Melissa S. James.)

When they find the book, you are likely to hear the following remark: "Oh, it is a print-on-demand book." They act like that means it has the black plague. Don't give them all the arguments about the pluses and minuses of various types of publishing. They already have their minds made up. Instead, turn it around to your advantage.

"Yes, that's right. That means you only have to order a couple of copies to see if they sell. You don't have to order a whole case of them like you do from the big publishers."

Touché! You have just scored the first point. Most managers aren't prepared for that kind of a response. It is time to move on.

"Is it returnable?"

This is one of those issues you might not agree with. If your publisher offers a *legitimate* return policy, it is well worth the money you will probably have to pay to make your book appeal to the big bookstores.

There are, as always, charlatans lurking who want to make a fast buck and offer the moon. If the returnability offer comes from a source outside your own publisher, be very careful and make sure that they really do what they say they will.

If your book is not returnable, especially if you are still in your regional bookstores, sometimes they will accept an alternative. Try this.

"Since the book has a good regional appeal, would you be willing to buy a few copies? Say maybe just 4 or 5? If they don't sell in 6 months, I will buy them back from you at the cost you paid for them. Chances are, if you get them from

Ingram, you will sell them within that length of time. What do you have to lose?"

While this is a business proposition you are involved in, a little humor goes ten miles compared to one mile of a "serious" approach. You might, at this time, add some comment like, "It is a really good book. Here is a review it got on Amazon.com." Hand them a printout of the review. Also, remember, Amazon is Barnes & Noble's biggest competitor! They don't want them to get ahead in the game.

To veer to the left for a moment, every review, every award, every comment by a "died-in-the-wool fan" is important in the field of sales. Use everything you have to your advantage.

When I use personal responses to some of these situations, it is because—when it comes to marketing to bookstores—the most frequently asked question I get asked is "What do you say to them?" All such references are done to prove a point, not to sell one of my books.

When I call a bookstore, usually while they are looking in the computer for the book in their database, I make a comment such as *"Par for the Course* was selected by *Affaire de Coeur* magazine as the best time-travel of 2003."

If the reception has been cool, at this point it *always* warms up. One little plug by somebody besides you—the author—is far more valuable than your own opinion. Everybody who ever writes a book thinks their book is the best thing since *Gone with the Wind*. When they see that somebody else thinks it is that good, you have just scored another point.

This is important: get as many people to review your books as you can. Keep a copy of those reviews handy when you approach the bookstores. Try to win prizes from legitimate contests (that does not mean the ones that you pay a fortune to enter). Every "good" thing you can gain on your book, the better your chances of being taken seriously become.

Going back to Melissa S. James' book *Stolen in the Storm,* reviewers have compared it to Mary Higgins Clark's books. So, when she calls bookstores she can honestly say, "A reviewer at MyShelf said it could give Mary Higgins Clark a real run for her money."

Have you ever gone to Amazon.com to see who they are comparing your books with? The people you are compared with are almost always somebody who is, at the very least, much better known than you are. For example, my mysteries have listed "People who bought these books also bought...John Grisham and James Patterson." It pays to see who people who like your books also like. Then you can tell the bookstore managers "People compare my book (insert name of book here) to... (fill in the blank)."

Once the manager has agreed to order "a couple of copies to see if they sell," ask if they can be placed in the "regional" section, rather than just haphazardly going here or there. In our local Barnes & Noble store, my books are placed in the regional section, but there are also a couple of copies in the proper section, by genre. The manager told me that for every copy they sell from the "mainstream shelves," they sell five copies from the regional section.

There are usually fewer titles in the regional section. Your competition is much less. You have a far better chance of your book being placed face forward instead of spine display. That makes a huge difference in how many people find it to look at it, and hopefully buy it.

That brings us to another matter. *People (especially bookstore people) DO judge a book by its cover.* Bookstore managers look for covers that stand out. Your chance of getting a high priority placement increases dramatically by having an outstanding, attractive cover. This, again, is something you should have thought about before your book was ever published. Fortunately, many print-on-demand or small press companies allow the author to either create, or at the very least approve their cover. So if your cover doesn't call for a sharp salute from the managers, you have no one but yourself to blame.

The next argument you might hear is, "The discount is so low that we won't stock it."

This is another one of those things you should have done before you selected a publisher. Some publishers (even print-on-demand or small traditional publishers) set the discount they offer the distributors from 10-25%. Look for a publisher that either has the discount at 40% (at the low end) or will allow you to set the discount yourself.

When you start out with your book, you can set the discount at 25% with no trouble. Why? Because the majority of your first sales will be to family and friends. These will probably be direct sales from you. In these cases, the discount doesn't matter. But if you plan to get into the bookstores, go back to your publisher and "renegotiate" your rate of discount. The big traditional publishers offer 55% to the distributors like Ingram and Baker & Taylor.

"But how will I make any money that way?" Stop and think about it a minute. If you sell five copies of your book at a 25% discount and make $2.50 per copy, but you sell five hundred copies by getting it into the bookstores, and you make $1.25 at a 50% discount...well, you figure it out.

Once you have successfully gotten your local bookstore to carry your book, even if it is just for a trial run, it is time to widen your horizon. It is time to move from Jerusalem to Judaea. When you contact the chain bookstores in your surrounding area, make sure you tell them that "the Barnes & Noble in _____ is carrying it, and it is selling quite well." (Make sure it is, before you say this. They can easily check.)

If they are hesitant, saying that you are not "in demand" in their area, even though you might be in your hometown, ask them if they will be willing to carry it if you get some publicity in their area.

Then get busy and call the radio stations (preferably either Talk Radio or NPR) to see if you can get an interview or two in their area. Call the newspaper in that area and see if you can get a review. If the paper has a policy against reviewing print-on-demand titles—and many newspapers, un-fortunately, do—try a different angle. If your book is a non-fiction "business-type" book, contact the person in charge of the business section and see if they will give you a brief note about "regional author has new book published." If it has a religious theme, try the person who writes that friendly little column about "Faith in our area." If it has a political vent, find out who writes the best op-ed articles. When a door closes, look for the closest open window.

After you have created some "hype" for your book, call the bookstore back again, letting them know when the radio program will air or when it will be in the newspaper. Your chances of getting them to order a few copies have increased greatly.

One of the most important issues to present to the bookstores is that this is not only a "print-on-demand" title, but it is a "print-IN-demand" book. If you can, in some way, convince them that many people are indeed ordering the book, they will listen with interest. If, for instance, you are trying to break the Barnes & Noble barrier, long before you approach the brick-and-mortar stores, direct potential customers to www.bn.com to purchase the books. The people who run the regular stores have easy access to the database that comes in from their on-line stores as well, so they are much more apt to stock a book that has sold one hundred copies from their brother outlet than a book that has sold two copies.

If you succeed in getting your book into any bookstores (at least I have found this to be true with Barnes & Noble, which is the chain I have dealt with primarily), there is a neat little secret that a bookstore manager from Louisiana told me. If you get two copies of your book on the shelves and they sell, the computer automatically orders four copies the next time around. Once those four sell, the computer orders eight copies. Then it goes to sixteen, and it stays at that sixteen level as long as the books continue to sell.

One of the arguments I have heard from authors is, "I can't travel from one town to another to try to sell my book. I have a full-time job...I have children...I am handicapped...I can't afford it..."

If you are looking for an excuse, you will find it. You don't have to look far. I can't travel far, either. I have a disabled husband. Does that stop me? No. Here is how I do it.

I buy a phone calling card from Sam's Club. I am not paid to advertise for them; they just have the cheapest cards available. For (at this time) 3.4 cents a minute, you can make calls to the bookstores, whether they are in Jerusalem (your home town), Judaea (your surrounding area) or the uttermost parts of the world (the entire USA). That means you can talk about 11½ minutes for the cost of one regular postage stamp. If you spend 3 minutes per call and even if you get one out of every three bookstores interested in your books, that's still a very good rate of return.

This sounds like blatant self-promotion, but I don't know any other way to do this. The question I am asked most often is "How do you approach the bookstores? When you get the manager on the phone, what do you say? I don't have a clue where to start."

Let me preface a typical conversation with a couple of things that should go without saying, but which are often overlooked. First, if you want the managers to be enthusiastic about your book, you have to ooze enthusiasm yourself.

Secondly, give them something that provides a reason to want the book. Does it have a certain holiday theme? Then call the stores at the appropriate time of year. Does your main character play golf or baseball? Use that as your "pitch." Is it a book about the Civil War? Find out where the Civil War battle reenactments are held and contact every one of those bookstores.

It is a well-established fact that non-fiction is easier to sell than fiction, so you have to work a bit harder at it. In non-fiction, try to find something "timely" about your book. Is the subject how to make wise investments? Use the Martha Stewart scandal. "I can tell your readers exactly how to stay out of prison and still make money on the stock market."

If somebody can make a *New York Times* bestseller out of a book on 101 ways to use duct tape, you can certainly make a success out of your book, no matter what the subject.

Here is a sample conversation from one of my calls to a "generic" chain bookstore about *Par for the Course*, my time travel.

Mgr.: "May I help you?"

Me: "I hope so. My name is Janet Smith, and I am an author. Unfortunately I live nowhere near you; I am in North Dakota. I would much rather be where you are."

Mgr.: "What can I do for you?"

Me: "I have a new book out that I am hoping you will be interested in carrying a couple of copies. I have the ISBN, if that's the easiest way for you to find it. It is distributed by both Ingram and Baker & Taylor." I then proceed to give him the ISBN. While he looks it up in the computer, I continue.

Me: "It is a time travel. It takes a modern young golfer back to the 1500s, where she gets to golf with Mary, Queen of Scots, who was the first woman golfer in history."

Mgr.: "I have it here. Oh, you have quite a few books. Are these all yours?"

Me: "Yes, I have 17 books out." I laugh a little as I add, "People say they are all good. In fact, *Par for the Course* was named by *Affaire de*

Coeur magazine readers as the best time travel of 2003."

Mgr.: "So I see by your cover that it has a golf theme? Everybody around here golfs. I'll order a couple of copies in and we'll see how it goes."

Me: "Thank you. If you would like, go to my web site at www.janetelainesmith.com and you can contact me through there. I'd be glad to send you some autographed bookplates to stick in them if you'd like."

Mgr.: "That would be great. I'm really glad you called about it. I'll check on some of your other books, too."

Me: "*Dunnottar* and *Marylebone* are the first two books in the 'Keith Trilogy.' *Par for the Course* is the final one. I hope you enjoy them. Again, thank you so much. Happy reading!"

Mgr.: "Will you let us know when your next book comes out? We'll take a look at it."

Is it an easy task? No way! Is it possible? Yes. Is it the end-all in book sales? That is open for discussion. But if you don't "make it" into the super-stores, don't give up and sit back, thinking nobody will ever find your book and you wonder why you ever wrote it. Everybody you know has already bought a copy.

Anything worth having costs something.

Chapter 3
INDEPENDENCE DAY

What if all your efforts to get your book into the chain bookstores fail? Are you doomed? Do you resort to a life of cyber-stores, hoping against hope that somebody stumbles across your masterpiece?

Take heart, my fellow authors! There are thousands of small independent bookstores that are just waiting to hear about great new books. There are several advantages that exist by being on their shelves. Here are just a few of them.

They do not *have to* put all the bestsellers on their shelves. Nobody gives the owner orders; he (or she) is their own boss.

They are always looking for something new and different.

They know their readers' tastes intimately.

They are interested in regional titles.

Your books are much more apt to get a front-face display, as they rotate the books more frequently.

If the owner decides he likes your book, he is very apt to "plug it" to his readers, especially his regular customers.

There are many directories on the Internet that will help you locate the independent bookstores. Later in this book you will find an "experiment" to help you with contacting these stores on the Internet.

You can also follow the same instructions as we gave you for the chain stores.

There is an NPR (National Public Radio) program called "Brain Brew." It is a program by two fellows who give small business people suggestions on how to be successful. Recently, I spoke with them about how to get my books to sell better. Their advice was this: Concentrate on the independent booksellers. If they are members of the American Booksellers Association, they list their books on www.booksense.com and when you contact the bookstore owners, ask them if they decide that they like your book, if they will nominate it for their "Top 76" choices. Those choices are the first books to be picked up by hundreds of other independent bookstores. And they aren't usually the ones that are on the *New York Times, Publishers' Weekly,* or *USA Today* lists. These are the books that their own customers have recommended. These are the books that are actually selling all across America. Your books might not be on those "big-name lists," but *they will be* some of the truly best-selling books in the country. What you want is not fame; what you want is fans.

Is this a sure-fire answer to seeing your books lining the shelves of at least some bookstores? If you really work at it, while the first effort might fail, I guarantee that you can make this one succeed. You just have to shift your priorities a bit.

As I often end some of my marketing columns in various magazines (both print and e-zines), Happy Sales to You!

Chapter 4
HOW TO BUILD A BETTER...

No, we don't want a better mousetrap, but we want to "catch" potential readers. We want to turn them into fans. Most authors today don't intend to write one book; they figure that while this might not be a self-sustaining job (at least at the onset), they enjoy the challenge of creating. Their minds work on overdrive most of the time. Their characters live in their heads long before they touch the paper or computer. Consequently, no effort is too small when it comes to creating that base of die-hard devotees. Do you think John Grisham or Dean Koontz envisioned the type of following they have today? Did Nora Roberts, when she started out, think she would be recognized when she dashed in to get a quart of milk? That could be you. The rest of the book is devoted to what have become known as "PromoPaks." They consist of twenty-eight easy-to-follow step-by-step instructions on how to get your book in "the flow" of today's readers. The majority of them won't cost you anything—except time and a computer connection or a phone calling card (which we have already discussed in Chapter 2.

Read these pages carefully. Then go back to the beginning and connect the dots, one at a time. When you have finished all of them, you will be much better prepared to move on to Chapters 2 and 3, getting your books onto the shelves where every Tom, Dick and Harry can see them, carry them to the checkout desk and go home to devour them.

Why will these simple procedures help? It is very simple. You will have solid proof that your book is not only printed-on-demand, but it is very heavily *in demand!* And that's what it's all about!

Chapter 5
REVIEWS

Like a review of opening night on Broadway, every author hopes for a rave review of their book. In the chapter on reviews we will discuss how to locate review sites on the Internet and how to contact reviewers in newspapers and magazines. Here we will delve deeper into how to tell when a review is going to help and when it will hinder the sale of your book. Also, we will show examples of how to zoom in on certain areas with the same book, giving different slants to suit the audience.

A bad review can do as much harm for an author and a book as a good review can help it. Some reviewers will not review a book they do not like. We should all hope to be as lucky as to get all of our reviews done by such a person. And just because one reviewer doesn't like your book does not mean it is a bad book; it simply means that their tastes and yours are not the same.

The following is an example of a good review. No, it is a *rave* review. What made it even better was that I did not know Richard Seltzer, the reviewer. I will give it to you in its entirety here for the purpose of showing you what to look for in your own reviews. Please bear with me.

HOUSE CALL TO THE PAST
By Janet Elaine Smith
Reviewed by Richard Seltzer for
samizdot.com

How could I resist the temptation of the story of a witch on Cape Cod?

We vacation at Harwich on the Cape for two weeks each summer, and the setting of Janet Elaine Smith's latest book, "House Call to the Past," is right next door—in Brewster and Yarmouth, in 1713 and 1992.

Before diving in, calibrate your expectations—this is a light, fun romance. There are sci-fi style time shifts from 1713 to 1992 and back again, but without sci-fi style explanation. In a thunderstorm, by simply walking across a field to help someone in evident distress, Dr. Angus McPhearson walks into the past. Just suspend your disbelief, as you do when watching a tape of "Brigadoon," which the good doctor was watching right before this scene.

Also, don't expect detailed descriptions of what it was like to live in 1713 in Massachusetts, and don't expect satiric contrasts between the lifestyles of then and now, a la "Connecticut Yankee in King Arthur's Court." Yes, you will occasionally be reminded that the lifestyles, beliefs, and expectations are different—but with a light touch. Here is the doctor wearing a jogging outfit and running shoes, with a Rolex watch on his wrist and a well-stocked medical bag walking into Yarmouth 280 years ago and being immediately accepted, and more or less fitting in. Often, the barriers he faces are ones of personality and knowledge rather than of time. Those differences aren't the focus of the story; they are its context. The focus is on the characters and what they say and do.

Just expect and enjoy a love story, with a twist—a doctor in 1992 falling in love with a 15-year-old purported witch in 1713.

When Angus arrives, summoned in the storm by Maria Hallett's father (who has an intriguing but unexplained understanding of how the time-shift works), Maria is an unwed mother giving birth to the son of pirate Sam Bellamy. Angus' medical skill saves her life and the life of her son. Then he almost immediately saves her from condemnation as a witch by offering to marry her. (Remember, this is romance—love at first sight.)

Much of the fun—and there's lots of fun here—comes from the interplay between Angus and his new bride. Angus adapts to his new time frame. Maria adapts to being married to this stranger, and the two of them cope with the looming menace of her son's father, Sam the pirate.

The dialogue moves fast, un-encumbered with pedantic realism, which would have made communication between the two of them difficult (imagine bumping into Cotton Mather on the street and striking up a conversation with him—the differences in vocabulary and grammar and accent). The plot moves along quickly too, focusing on their relationship first, Sam the pirate second, her family third, and, last of all, the minor challenges posed by the time difference.

Maria is presented as an enticing, quick-witted, playful, flirt. She has no magical powers other than her beauty and youth and vivacity. Thanks to the intervention of Angus, the townsfolk shift from considering her as a malevolent witch—a dangerous label at a time not that long after the events in Salem—to using the term "witch" in her presence playfully, almost as a compliment, as we might do today, with someone who is "enchanting" and "casts spells" on men.

If anyone has "magical" power, it is Maria's father, who was able to summon Angus through time, and who, without ever discussing such matters with him, understands that Angus can and must return to his own time.

As explained in the author's note at the end, Smith is a descendant of the historical Maria Hallett. And Maria's story has been told on the Discovery Channel, in National Geographic articles, and in Readers' Digest. In those versions, Maria is considered a witch.

Smith explains, "Since she was an ancestor of mine, I figured it was my forte to redeem her."

But this Maria needs no redemption. She's simply delightful—witch or no witch. I look forward to the promised sequel, "Port Call to the Future."

(Seltzer, a free-lance reviewer, can be reached at seltzer@samizdat.com or via www.samizdat.com.)

That, to me, is a great review. Why? First, it is exciting. You can feel the reviewer's passion for the story. He is not just "reporting," he is "sharing a feeling" for the book.

Second, he makes the story interesting without giving away too much of the plot. This is critical in a review; if a reviewer spoils the story line, as in a joke when you blurt out the punch line too soon, you will lose almost all the readers that review might "hook." Third and last, the review draws the reader into the story, wanting them to know more.

But first you have to figure out how to get people to review your book. It is not as difficult as it sounds. You do not have to pay money or promise return favors, just go about it systematically.

Step 1. *Anyone who likes your book can write a review*.

If you hear from a reader who has great things to say about your book, ask them if they would post a review for you. The most logical places are at online bookstores such as Amazon.com, bn.com, booksamillion.com and many others. Anyone can post their opinions at these places. It is free, and such popular sites are looked at by thousands of people daily. An Amazon employee who works with the Advantage Program said that every time a 5 star review goes up on amazon.com for a book, the sales raise on the average by 13%. To accomplish this, use your friends and family. If you have lots of siblings and they all support your writing, get them to write a review on these sites.

Step 2. *Post your book reviews where others have the most to gain.*

Who is that? Obviously, it is your publisher. Every time one of your books is sold, you make money. So does your publisher. If your publisher has an online bookstore or even a promotional site, get them to put at least the best quotes from your reviews on there.

Step 3. *Gear your reviews towards the geographical areas that are apt to have the most interest in your book.*

If your book is set in some specific locale, the newspapers there are almost always not only willing, but anxious to run a review on it. Make sure you know when it will run so you can contact the bookstores in that area so they will be sure to have the book in stock when the review runs. Bookstores that under normal circumstances will not carry POD books, if they know it will be reviewed locally, will rescind their decision and stock your title.

Step 4. *Contact regional magazines.*

They will not give you a free ad for your book, but they will almost always do a book review that they think will appeal to their readership. Be sure you furnish them with a copy of the cover to include in the review, even if they agree to read the book from a pdf file. It is a good idea to also discuss the book with the editor. Many of them will include some of the thoughts of the author, particularly why you happened to set the book in their back yard.

Step 5. *Furnish copies of other favorable reviews to the newspapers you contact.*
Newspapers and magazines both want to look good in the eyes of their peers. If neighboring (or other larger) periodicals have reviewed your book, they want to jump on the bandwagon. The more reviews you get, the more reviews you can get.

Step 6. *Aim high*.
Once you have numerous reviews in newspapers, suggest to your local newspaper editor (or book editor) that they try to get it onto the AP or UPI. This is especially appropriate if your book has some timely subject, such as the Sept. 11 terrorist attack or the sending of the troops to Afghanistan or the plunging of the stock market or any number of other subjects.

Step 7. *Get as many on-line reviews as you can*.
Once again, it is time to go to your favorite search engine (google.com happens to be mine) and do a search for "Book review sites." Begin contacting them by e-mail, giving some "hook" that is likely to catch their attention. One way to capture that attention is to use your favorite quote from the book. If your characters are especially appealing, concentrate on that.

Reviewers get dozens of requests to review books every week. You have to make yours special to get them to agree to look at it. Scope out their sites before you contact them. If you have a sweet romance and all of the books they have reviewed are horrors or thrillers, they probably will pass on your book. If you want to make it easier, narrow your search to "romance book review sites," "mystery review sites," "how-to book review sites," etc. Then begin assaulting each and every one of them.

Step 8. *Contact writers groups you belong to, letting them know that your book is available for review.*

Many of the people who belong to such groups do reviews or have web sites of their own that post book reviews.

Step 9. *Find online groups that list books that are available for review.*

One of the primary places to find such groups is at www.yahoogroups.com. Once there, scroll down to "arts and entertainment" then click on "books" and then on to "reviews." There are numerous groups set up specifically for this purpose, such as Post-A-Page and Reviewers Choice. Join these groups and put the information they will allow on your books. Reviewers do scan these sites to see what is there.

Step 10. *Keep your reviews handy*.

Keep a copy of your most current (or your best) reviews in your purse, your wallet or your briefcase. When the conversation turns to your book (and doesn't it always?), be like a Boy Scout: be prepared. "I just happen to have a review with me!" serves quite well. This accomplishes two things: it builds the interest in your book, with the possibility of a future sale, and it creates interest (and a good dose of ego!) in you as an author, so when your next book comes out and that person just happens to run across a review, they will go out and buy the book, then boast to all their friends, "I *know* that author."

This is by no means a complete list, but here are some excellent book review spots to get you started. You can find their addresses either online or at your local public library. You can find thousands more at your favorite search engine.

<u>Print Reviews</u>:
New York Times
Washington Post
Boston Globe
Midwest Book Review
Mystery Readers Journal
Danny Reviews
Romantic Times
CNN Book Reviews
Chronicle Book Reviews

On-line Review sites:

There are many, but there is one that is so comprehensive that it will lead you to dozens of other sites. The great thing about this site is that you can search internally by genre, which review sites will accept e-books and pdf's. With this site, you don't need any others.

http://www.bookconnector.com

Online self-reviews:
www.published.com
www.allreaders.com

Chapter 6
CHATS

One of the best ways to get yourself "known" among the world of readers is to enter the cyber-world of chats. You can start out by just attending chats of other authors. When the opportunity arises, you can always refer to your own book. Soon people will begin asking you about your book and your own writing, and before long you will discover that the people who run or moderate the chats will come pounding at your door, asking if you would like to be a guest author. That means, basically, that you are the "big cheese." People want to know about YOU—the author. This is your time to shine—and to sell books.

Step 1. *Locate authors/readers chats.*
If you are a member of any authors' e-groups (and if you aren't, you should be), send an e-mail to them and ask them if they know of any chats for authors or readers. Go to a search engine and do a search on author chats.

Step 2. *Start attending as a guest.*

Make yourself known to the groups you are visiting. It is fine to "chat hop," but you will become more known and (usually) respected if you stick with a few smaller chats to begin with. This builds an interested audience in your book.

Step 3. *Offer your services.*

After you are very familiar with the moderator of the chat, contact him/her privately and let them know you are available as a guest author. You will endear yourself to them in extra measure if you offer to be a "fill-in" on a moment's notice if the scheduled guest doesn't show up.

Step 4. *Be free-flowing in your conversation.*

Whether you are just attending a chat or if you are the guest author, make every effort to be sure the "conversation" doesn't lag. There is nothing more frustrating than to sit at a chat where nobody says anything. If there is a lull (it is called "dead air"), follow the old tried-and-trued advice to "seize the day." A moderator will be grateful for your help.

Step 5. *Be creative.*

You are a writer. Once you are a guest author, put that creativity to work for you. One of the first things you will be asked is to describe your book. Remember how you had to use a "hook" to get that editor's attention? It is just as important to capture the attention of your prospective readers.

Step 6. *Let them know where to find you.*

Before you leave the chat, or even more importantly before the guests start leaving, make sure you have given them your e-mail address, your web site url and where they can buy your books. Offer to send them an autographed bookplate if they contact you after they have purchased the book. If you are running a contest on your web site, be sure to encourage them to enter. This not only gives you the knowledge of who they are, but provides you with a way to contact them when your next book comes out.

Step 7. *Be courageous; launch out on your own.*

When you have garnered a fair amount of readers, announce your own chat to discuss your book. You can do this for the book that is out now, and you can also throw out a "teaser" about upcoming books. When you are in charge, it is up to you to make sure the conversation flows smoothly. If you don't have dozens of people at the first few chats, don't worry about it. Word spreads as time goes by.

Step 8. *Get your own "house" where people can visit you.*

This perhaps should have come earlier, but if you have not set up a chat room at your web site, you must do it now. You can always "borrow" someone else's chatroom, but you will find that it becomes familiar territory if it is always "at your house." There are numerous free chat rooms available. Just go to your favorite search engine again and enter a search for "free chat rooms." I have mine at www.bravenet.com but there are many others available, too.

Step 9. *Practice!*

Several days ahead of the scheduled chat, get a friend to meet you in your chatroom for a "dry run." You want to be sure everything is in working order so you aren't caught on the day of the actual chat with a technical problem. If you do have trouble, most technical support from where you obtained your chat room is good about helping explain or correct the problem.

Okay, you are off and running. Have a good visit. Don't forget to bring the food and drinks along. Everybody loves to party!

Chapter 7
SERVICE CLUBS, ETC.

Organized groups of people who have like-minded goals present an often- overlooked opportunity to do book promotion. Here is how you take the bull by the horns (or the Eagle by the beak or the Lion by the mane) and work your way into their hearts and pocketbooks. Just follow these simple steps to success:

Step 1. *Call your local Chamber of Commerce and ask for a list of the service clubs in your area.*

This list will probably include the name and phone number of the contact person and the place and time of each meeting.

Step 2. *Look through the list to see if there is anyone you know.*

If so, start there. That provides you a common denominator, making it easier if you are short in the self-esteem department.

Step 3. *Look for the purposes of the groups as listed.*

If you can find a key in your book which might tie in to the group's purpose, begin there. For example, if there is a reference to child abuse in your plotline, contact the Exchange Club, which is their primary goal of service.

Step 4. *Formulate your plan.*

Remember, many of these groups meet weekly. That means that they are always looking for new program ideas. Play on that fact.

Step 5. *Call the contact person, offering your services and set up a time for the meeting.*

Be sure to find out how long they want you to speak.

Step 6. *Make sure you have plenty of copies of your book to take with you.*

Step 7. *Take bookmarks, postcards, etc.*

This is so people who don't buy a copy of your book "on the spot" will not forget the name of the book (and your name) so they can purchase it later.

Step 8. *Open the meeting for questions and answers before the end of the meeting.*

You are probably a beginning author, but to the members of the group, you are a celebrity. Be prepared for sharing openly with them.

Step 9. *If possible, offer them a small discount on your book.*

This makes them feel "special," and it is surprising how many people can't resist a bargain.

Step 10. *Be prompt.*

Make sure you quit on time. Most of these people have jobs they have to get back to. If you make them late for work, they will never ask you back when your next book comes out.

Step 11. *It never hurts to send a thank you note after-the-fact.*

Not only will it endear you to the group, but that way your name goes into the minutes of the next meeting, too. Familiarity never hurts in the game of books and salesmanship.

Step 12. *If the group has a library (like the DAR, genealogy groups, Kem Temple, etc. often do) donate one copy of your book to the library.*

The following is by no means a complete list of service clubs, fraternities and sororities, but it is a beginning. To find such groups in your area, watch the listings in your local newspaper in the calendar of events. These groups are always looking for interesting programs; you are helping them as much as they are helping you. If it is possible to fit your book to their field of interest (some which are included here) you have a double plus in approaching them. Remember, if you make your presentation interesting—in other words, if you are enthusiastic about your books and your writing—word will quickly spread from one group to another and you will find yourself in demand as a speaker. No, they will probably not pay you and if you try to charge them for your services you will squash your chances for future engagements before you get a good start. But these people *do read* and they *do buy books*. And that is the name of the game.

SERVICE CLUBS:
Lions International—Motto: We serve
Rotary Clubs
Sertoma—speech and hearing disorders, promote freedom, tend to local needs
Toastmasters—to improve communications by their members
Kiwanis—serving the children of the world
Daughters of the American Revolution (DAR) – preserving history
Eagles—heart, kidney, diabetes, cancer; neglected and abused children and elderly; started Father's Day
Knights of Columbus (Catholic by origin)— dedicated to charity, unity, fraternity, patriotism and family life
Exchange Club—prevention of child abuse
Optimists—support youth
Shriners (Free Masons)—children's physical needs

Sons of Norway—preservation of Norwegian and Viking history

Veterans of Foreign War—military assistance and interest

Disabled American Veterans—military disabilities and handicaps

Elks

Eagles

General Federation of Women's Clubs—support the arts, preserve natural resources, promote education, encourage healthy lifestyles, stress civic involvement, work toward world peace and understanding

American Business Women's Association

Business and Professional Women's Clubs

Christian Women's Clubs

Quota—to promote reading

Eastern Star

SORORITIES AND FRATERNITIES:

Rather than try to identify all of these college-affiliated groups, we will direct you to a web site. Go to http://greekpages.com/org where you will find a current list of over 700 different sororities and fraternities. This site is a good, dependable one which has been in existence for quite some time, and it is updated fairly regularly. If you live in or near a college town, by all means check out these places. Besides being good readers, you might tap into a fair amount of aspiring writers as well. One of the best ploys for such an audience is to say, "If you want to know how I did it, the best way is to read my book." This might even open a door to future workshops at these organizations where you can provide help to a very captive audience.

Chapter 8
ONLINE CHAT INTERVIEWS

Every time you are interviewed about your book or your writing, the questions are almost always the same. *How do you get your ideas? When did you start writing? How are your sales?*

Many of these interviews are now conducted over the Internet by e-mail. But, I am here to tell you that there is a new and improved way to conduct an interview. Of course you, the author, are the interviewee, not the interviewer. But, let's walk through this with a step-by-step tutorial of how to get online chat interviews.

At the end, we will discuss the advantages of this system of interviewing, rather than the traditional "stodgy" way.

Step 1. *Get acquainted with various writers' web sites.*

Step 2. *Aim for the smaller, newer sites*.
They are always looking for fresh new ideas to make their sites stand out above the others that are out there.

Step 3. *Make yourself available to the webmaster.*
Offer to do some writing. Yes, do it for free. Each time you do this, you are creating interest in your writing. Each time you do this, your name is added to the search engines in another spot.

Step 4. *Suggest an alternate way of doing the interview.*
Make your characters available to answer the questions for you. Nobody knows you like they do; after all, they are your creation.

Why is this method of interviewing more interesting than the same old drudgery of a "normal" interview? It is simply because it is easy for you to steer the answers in the direction you want them to go. If the questions are boring and repetitive, that just calls for you to use more creativity in your answers.

Also, it is easy for you to spread the word to your friends, family members, e-groups, etc. that the interview is available. They can easily read it, and it doesn't cost them anything to get it, as it would in a print magazine. Besides, not all print magazines are available everyplace.

In most cases, you are not edited nearly as severely as you would be in a print magazine. You can be yourself, and "let your hair down," as it were. And as I have told you many times before in the PromoPaks, don't forget to have fun while you are doing it.

Chapter 9
HOW TO PREPARE AN EFFECTIVE PRESS RELEASE

Step 1. *Identify your geographical target.*

Start with where you are. People know you; that gives you a head start. The best place to start selling your books is in your own back yard. Get a state map and draw a ring around a 50-mile or 100-mile radius from your hometown, depending on how far you want to travel on the first leg of your publicity tour. Check in local phone books for these newspapers so when you have your press release ready to send out you can begin the marketing at home.

With a paper and pen in hand, try reliving your life. Write down every place that you have lived, no matter for how short a time. Write down one good thing you remember happening while you lived there.

Write down the location of your book. This is particularly true if your book is fictional. If the location is fictional, in what part of the country is it set? Is it near a fairly large city?

Now that you have your list of places where there is a natural tie-in to your book, take your list of newspapers and highlight each of the newspapers in that area.

Now that you have that done, let's get to the nitty-gritty of starting the actual review. Since each of you has a different story to tell, we will use circumstances in my own life and build a review for my young adult book, *My Dear Phebe,* using just one location to start with.

The following is the beginning of the press release:

Janet Elaine Smith, well-known author, genealogist and historian, has penned a book, My Dear Phebe, *which focuses in part on one of her favorite parts of the country: Pennsylvania. Smith spent a year at the WEC International headquarters in Ft. Washington, PA before going to Venezuela, SA as a missionary. During her time here, she spent one fine Sunday afternoon going through the battlefields at Gettysburg and later spent perhaps the most memorable afternoon of her life with Mamie and "Ike" Eisenhower.*

You think your life is not nearly as exciting? Go back and look at what you wrote about one of the places you have lived. It might be something a simple as "he/she attended school at ..." or "where his father was on the school board..." or "who fondly remembers visiting the swimming pool when he/she was a child..." If your book takes place somewhere you have never been, perhaps you could include a statement such as "Rolling Hills, Tennessee has always held a fascination for the writer. 'In this way, I can at least imagine that I live in such a beautiful place.'" You have captured your targeted audience with no prior connection to them whatsoever.

Step 2. *Find your tie-in.*

Is your book a fictional one? Is it historical? If so, if you have done your research well, the tie-in should be obvious. Most historical novels begin with a "real" event. Write it down on a piece of paper. *My Dear Phebe* deals with the Civil War. How can the Civil War present a tie-in to today, especially as a young-adult book, as it is? Simple, it deals with the feelings of children towards war. That is its biggest selling point: teachers and parents are encouraged to buy it and read it with their children to open up the lines of communication about the terrorist attack on America on Sept. 11, 2001. A stretch? It is simply being in the right place at the right time. While it is certainly not intended to make a bad situation worse, it might never have caught the eye of the media at any other time.

Is your book contemporary fiction? What about the story line makes it fit a specific readership? Does it involve golf? Locate the golf circuit in your area. You can branch out later. Maybe it is a mystery which involves a bed-and-breakfast setting. Tom Sawyer and Huckleberry Finn would have been a sure bet for men who were fishermen, if only as a hobby. *Gone With the Wind* was perfect for Civil War enthusiasts. Again, write down the topic that is foremost in your book.

What if your book is a nonfiction volume? Maybe you have a do-it-yourself book on repairing furnaces. You have a perfect target area in the north country, where the functioning of a furnace is literally a matter of life and death. Does it deal with dog breeding? Fashion? Cooking? Gardening? Whatever your topic, write it down. Use your imagination. After all, you are a writer, and all writers are creative. You have a book about tulips or windmills or clogs? Send it to Holland, Michigan! It is the perfect market spot.

Let's progress to the next section of our review of *My Dear Phebe.*

Smith's book, My Dear Phebe, *is based on actual letters that were sent to 10-year-old Phebe Irvine, who lived in Sault Ste. Marie,*

Michigan during the Civil War. The letters were written by Phebe's uncle, James Irvine, who lived in Gettysburg, PA.

We have here the tie-in to the story line. Just for fun, let's return to the book about tulips. Let's create a tie-in for our Holland, Michigan newspaper.

John Doe's book, Tulips and Two Lips: How They Lead to Love, *will show you some of the most romantic ways you can use tulips in wooing and winning that perfect woman you have been eyeing. Holland, Michigan, the U.S. counterpart to Amsterdam, is certainly going to unlock the secrets that bloom so profusely in their back yard every spring.*

Yes, that book is (probably) non-existent. But if you can sell a book like that, just imagine how much easier it would be to sell your book.

Step 3. *Establish the relevance of your book to today's readers.*

Stop and ponder for a few moments the best way your book would fit the needs of today's audience. If you have a mystery, has something in the news recently sent shivers up and down your spine because it is so much like your book? Use it! Tom Clancy is a master at this. Call it dumb luck or fate or whatever you want to, but his books are so close to what often happens in our world that the government has called him in for questioning. If you have a non-fiction book on a topic, how can it make a better world? If you have a book on money-saving tips, use the fact that there are massive employment cutbacks because of the now famous "9-11" attack and you can help thousands of Americans survive with lower incomes. Suppose you have something as everyday ordinary as a cookbook, but you have little "feel good" quips throughout the book. Never before have American families been so aware of how important family is. Put your marketing talents to use by praising its value to share a few minutes of "togetherness" around the dinner table, suggesting that families read the quote for the recipe Mom (or Dad) has prepared for the meal.

Again, turning to *My Dear Phebe,* we have already touched on how timely the book is. Here is how to use that information in your review:

My Dear Phebe touches a nerve in all of today's children. One youngster, after watching the airplanes crash into the World Trade Towers remarked, "There were so many planes and so many big buildings!" It is hard to imagine what our children felt as they viewed the events that horrified all Americans. This book will open the airwaves between children and their parents and teachers so the healing process can begin. Only as fears are faced and expressed can they be resolved.

Let's go back to our make-believe book, *Tulips and Two Lips,* again. Here is a fun, catchy section for that review.

In the wake of complex matters that fill the airwaves every day, is there an escape? Sometimes the answers lie in the simplest things. Tulips and Two Lips *demonstrates how to overcome frustration and fear by sharing a simple flower, the love of gardening and romance of today's distraught people.*

Step 4. *Prove your qualifications for writing your book.*

If you want to make believers out of the general public, you have to convince them that nobody else could have written your book. You were unquestionably the best candidate to produce the finished product.

Think back to the moment that the inspiration hit you to write a book. *Your* book. At that moment, you were the world's best expert on your subject. Now all you have to do is to convince the readers of the world that you know what you are talking (or writing) about.

Write down the experience you have in the field about which you are writing. If it is fiction, this is a little tougher than with nonfiction. Still, there has to be some reason why you chose to write this specific book. It's time to drag that out and put it on the clothesline for everyone to see.

With *My Dear Phebe,* it is easy to establish myself with my credentials. Phebe is my own flesh and blood. She is family. Well, okay, so she is a "shirttail relative," but that still means that I have the right to tell her story.

If your book is nonfiction, this is probably easier to do. Let's go back to our imaginary book, *Tulips and Two Lips*. Have you raised tulips for years? Was it your grandmother's passion and you inherited the love of these delightful bulbous beauties from her? Is your heritage Dutch and you just have an inbred penchant for them? Since the book deals with "romance on a budget," you might include a bit of humor (which never hurts!) such as "I won my wife by convincing her that a bouquet of dandelions—picked by my own loving hands—was much more romantic and meaningful than three dozen roses."

As our press release of *My Dear Phebe* continues, we add:

Smith has a special interest in the history of My Dear Phebe, *as the actual character, Phebe Irvine, is Smith's great-grandfather's mother-in-law (by a second marriage). Smith was given Phebe's letters from Uncle James by her step-great uncle, Ross Hallett. This is one of Smith's "personal" fictional efforts, as was her previous* House Call to the Past, *which was based on the life of another Hallett ancestor, Maria Hallett, who was accused of witchcraft in the early 1700's. Smith is also the author of the award-winning bestseller* Dunnottar, *which is based on her husband's Keith lineage. Having spent over 20 years as a genealogist, she often draws on her genealogical findings (both her own and others) to spin her yarns.*

Now we have the finished product. Here is the press release.

Janet Elaine Smith, well-known author, genealogist and historian, has penned a book, My Dear Phebe, *which focuses on one of her favorite parts of the country: Pennsylvania. Smith spent a year at the WEC International headquarters in Ft. Washington, PA before going to Venezuela, SA as a missionary. During her time here she spent one fine Sunday afternoon going through the battlefields at Gettysburg and later spent perhaps the most memorable afternoon of her life with Mamie and "Ike" Eisenhower.*

Smith's book, My Dear Phebe, *is based on actual letters that were sent to 10-year-old Phebe Irvine, who lived in Sault Ste. Marie, Michigan during the Civil War. The letters were written by Phebe's uncle, James Irvine, who lived in Gettysburg, PA.*

My Dear Phebe *touches a nerve in all of today's children. One youngster, after watching the airplanes crash into the World Trade Towers remarked, "There were so many planes and so many big buildings!" It is hard to imagine what our children felt as they viewed the events that horrified all Americans. This book will open the airwaves between children and their parents and teachers so the healing process can begin. Only as fears are faced and expressed can they be resolved.*

Smith has a special interest in the history of My Dear Phebe, *as the actual character, Phebe Irvine, is Smith's great-grandfather's mother-in-law (by a second marriage). Smith was given Phebe's letters from Uncle James by her step-great uncle, Ross Hallett. This is one of Smith's "personal" fictional efforts, as was her previous* House Call to the Past, *which was based on the life of another Hallett ancestor, Maria Hallett, who was accused of witchcraft in the early 1700's. Smith is also the author of the award-winning bestseller,* Dunnottar, *which is based on her husband's Keith lineage. Having spent over 20 years as a genealogist, she often draws on her genealogical findings (both her own families and others) to spin her popular yarns.*

Using the same principles, create your own press release and you are ready to go.

Now that the creative side of the press release is done, it is time to get to the technical part of it: actually sending it to the newspapers, radio stations, magazines, etc.

Step 1. *Take your newspaper list, which you have received with this Article, and mark the geographical areas where you feel you will have the most interest.*

Start locally, then move to the setting of the book, then to a wider area.

Step 2. *By simply typing in the URL for each targeted newspaper, you will go directly to their web site.*
Locate their e-mail address and put it on a separate entry on a floppy disk so you can create your own personalized mailing list.

Step 3. *Return to your completed press release.*

Step 4. *Go to <edit> and highlight the entire press release.*

Step 5. *Click on <cut>.*

Step 6. *Take the list of e-mail addresses you have created and go to your e-mail server.*

Step 7. *Enter the addresses in "Send to" and then put your mouse so it is at the beginning of the body of your message.*

Step 8. *Type in "Press release" on your subject line.*

Step 9. *Go to <edit> on your toolbar and click on <paste>.*

Step 10. *Hit "send" on your e-mail and you are on your way. You have just sent your press release to all those* *newspapers and you didn't even have to pay any postage.*

Here's a bonus for you. It's free! Use it.

State Newspaper Links for press releases:

ALABAMA
The Birmingham Post-Herald
http://www.postherald.com
Montgomery Advertiser
http://www.montgomeryadvertiser.com
Jacksonville News
http://www.jaxnews.com

ALASKA
Anchorage Daily News
http://www.and.com
Fairbanks Daily News
http://www.localnet.abracat.com/fairbanks
Juneau Empire
http://www.juneauempire.com

ARIZONA
The Arizona Republic
http://www.azcentral.com
Arizona Daily Star
http://www.azstarnet.com
Arizona Daily Sun
http://www.azdailysun.com

ARKANSAS
Arkansas Democrat Gazette
http://www.ardemgaz.com
Northwest Arkansas Times
http://www.nwarktimes.com
Newport Independent
http://www.newportindependent.com

CALIFORNIA
Los Angeles Times
http://www.latimes.com
San Francisco Chronicle
http://www.sfgate.com/chronicle
The Sacramento Bee
http://www.sacbee.com

COLORADO
Denver Rocky Mountain News
http://www.rockymountainnews.com
The Denver Post
http://www.denverpost.com
The Gazette
http://www.gazette.com

CONNECTICUT
The Stamford Advocate
http://www.stamfordadvocate.com
Hartford Advocate
http://www.hartfordadvocate.com
The Connecticut Post
http://www.connpost.com

DELAWARE

Dover Post
http://www.doverpost.com
Newark Post
http://www.ncbe.com/post
News Journal
http://www.delawareonline.com/newsjournal

FLORIDA

The Miami Herald
http://www.miamiherald.com/herald
The Orlando Sentinel
http://www.orlandosentinel.com
Jacksonville Times Union
http://www.jacksonville.com

GEORGIA

Atlanta-Journal Constitution
http://www.accessatlanta.com/ajc
Savannah Morning News
http://www.savannahnow.com
The Macon Telegraph
http://www.macontelegraph.com

HAWAII

Honolulu Advertiser
http://www.honoluluadvertiser.com
The Maui News
http://www.mauinews.com
Hawaii Tribune-Herald
http://www.hilohawaiitribune.com

IDAHO

The Idaho Statesman
http://www.idahostatesman.com
Moscow-Pullman Daily News
http://www.dnews.com
Lewiston Tribune
http://www.lmtribune.com

ILLINOIS

Chicago Tribune
http://www.chicagotribune.com
Chicago Sun-Times
http://www.suntimes.com
State Journal-Register
http://www.sj-r.com

INDIANA

Journal Gazette
http://www.journalgazette.com
The Indianapolis Star
http://www.indystar.com

IOWA

Des Moines Register
http://www.dmregister.com
Iowa City Press-Citizen
http://www.press-citizen.com
The Quad City Times
http://www.qctimes.com

KANSAS

Topeka Capital-Journal
http://www.cjonline.com
Kansas City Kansan
http://www.kansascitykansan.com
The Leavenworth Times
http://www.leavenworthtimes.com

KENTUCKY

Lexington Herald-Leader
http://www.kentuckyconnect.com/
The Richmond Register
http://www.richmondregister.com
Bowling Green Daily News
http://www.bgdailynews.com

LOUISIANA

The Shreveport Times
http://www.shreveporttimes.com
New Orleans Times Picayune
http://www.nola.com
Monroe News Star
http://www.thenewsstar.com

MAINE

Bangor Daily News
http://www.bangornews.com
Kennebec Journal
http://www.centralmaine.com
Portland Press Herald
http://www.portland.com

MARYLAND
The Baltimore Sun
http://www.sunspot.net
The Daily Record
http://www.mddailyrecord.com
Frederick News-Post
http://www.fredericknewspost.com

MASSACHUSETTS
The Boston Globe
http://www.boston.com/globe
The Boston Herald
http://www.bostonherald.com
The Salem News
http://www.salemnews.com

MICHIGAN
The Detroit News
http://www.detnews.com
Lansing State Journal
http://www.lansingstatejournal.com
The Detroit Free Press
http://www.freep.com

MINNESOTA
Minneapolis Star Tribune
http://www.startribune.com
St. Paul Pioneer Planet
http://www.pioneerplanet.com
The Duluth News-Tribune
http://www.duluthnews.com

MISSISSIPPI

Biloxi Sun Herald
http://www.sunherald.com
Jackson Clarion Ledger
http://www.clarionledger.com
The Vicksburg Post
http://www.vicksburgpost.com

MISSOURI

Kansas City Star
http://www.kcstar.com
Jackson Co. Examiner
http://www.examiner.net
The Joplin Globe
http://www.joplinglobe.com

MONTANA

The Billings Gazette
http://www.billingsgazette.com
The Missoulian
http://www.missoulian.com
Butte Montana Standard
http://www.mtstandard.com

NEBRASKA

Lincoln Journal Star
http://www.journalstar.com
The Columbus Telegram
http://www.columbustelegram.com
Norfolk Daily News
http://www.norfolkdailynews.com

NEVADA

Las Vegas Sun
http://lasvegassun.com
Las Vegas Review Journal
http://www.lvrj.com
Reno Gazette-Journal
http://www.rgj.com

NEW HAMPSHIRE

Concord Monitor
http://www.concordmonitor.com
The Eagle Times
http://www.eagle-times..com
Franklin Telegram
http://www.nnsweb.com

NEW JERSEY

Jersey Journal
http://www.nj.com/jjournal
The Trentonian
http://www.trentonian.com
Hackensack-The Record
http://www.bergen.com

NEW MEXICO

The Albuquerque Tribune
http://www.abqtrib.com
The Albuquerque Journal
http://www.abqjournal.com
Santa Fe New Mexican
http://www.sfnewmexican.com

NEW YORK
The Buffalo News
http://www.buffalo.com
New York Times
http://www.nytimes.com
Albany Times Union
http://www.timesunion.com

NORTH CAROLINA
Raleigh News & Observer
http://www.newsobserver.com
The Fayetteville Observer
http://www.fayettevillenc.com
The Charlotte Observer
http://www.charlotte.com

NORTH DAKOTA
Bismarck Tribune
http://www.bismarcktribune.com
Grand Forks Herald
http://www.grandforks.com
Fargo Forum
http://www.new.in-forum.com

OHIO
Cincinnati Post
http://www.cincypost.com
Akron Beacon Journal
http://www.ohio.com/bj
Medina Gazette
http://www.medina-gazette.com

OKLAHOMA

Tulsa World
http://www.tulsaworld.com
The Daily Oklahoman
http://www.newsok.com
Clinton Daily News
http://www.clintondailynews.com

OREGON

Portland Oregonian
http://www.oregonlive.com
The Bend Bulletin
http://www.bendbulletin.com
Medford Mail Tribune
http://www.mailtribune.com

PENNSYLVANIA

Philadelphia Daily News
http://www.phillynews.com
Pittsburgh Post-Gazette
http://www.post-gazette.com
The Scranton Times
http://www.scrantontimes.com

RHODE ISLAND

Providence Journal
http://www.projo.com
Pawtucket Times
http://www.pawtuckettimes.com
The Westerly Sun
http://www.westerlysun.com

JANET ELAINE SMITH

SOUTH CAROLINA
Charleston Post & Courier
http://www.charleston.net
Columbia—The State
http://www.thestate.com
The Island Packet
http://www.islandpacket.com

SOUTH DAKOTA
Rapid City Journal
http://www.rapidcityjournal.com
Sioux Falls Argus Leader
http://www.argusleader.com
Mitchell Daily Republic
http://www.mitchellrepublic.com

TENNESSEE
Memphis Commercial Appeal
http://www.gomemphis.com
Knoxville News-Sentinel
http://www.knownews.com
Nashville Tennessean
http://www.tennessean.com

TEXAS
Dallas Morning News
http://www.dallasnews.com
San Antonio Express News
http://www.mysanantonio.com/expressnews
Houston Chronicle
http://www.chron.com

UTAH
Salt Lake Tribune
http://www.sltrib.com
Provo Daily Herald
http://www.daily-herald.com
Ogden Standard-Examiner
http://www.standard.net

VERMONT
Burlington Free Press
http://www.burlingtonfreepress.com
Valley News
http://www.vnews.com
Bennington Banner
http://www.benningtonbanner.com

VIRGINIA
Richmond Times-Dispatch
http://www.timesdispatch.com
Charlottesville Daily Progress
http://www.dailyprogress.com
The Roanoke Times
http://www.roanoke.com

WASHINGTON
Seattle Post Intelligencer
http://www.seattlepi.nwsource.com
The Everett Herald
http://www.heraldnet.com
The Spokesman Review
http://www.spokesmanreview.com

WEST VIRGINIA
The Charleston Gazette
http://www.wvgazette.com
Charleston Daily Mail
http://www.dailymail.com
Huntington Herald Dispatch
http://www.herald-dispatch.com

WISCONSIN
Green Bay News-Chronicle
http://www.greenbaynewschron.com
Milwaukee Journal Sentinel
http://www.jsonline.com
Wisconsin State Journal
http://www.wisconsinstatejournal.com

WYOMING
Casper Star Tribune
http://www.trib.com
The Sheridan Press
http://www.thesheridanpress.com
Cheyenne Wyoming News
http://www.wyomingnews.com

Chapter 10
1-2-3 HOW-TO'S OF FAMILY HISTORY

So you want to write your family history, but you aren't sure where to begin. This is by no means a complete guide on how to find your entire family tree, but it is enough to get you off to a good start. Follow these easy steps and you are well on your way.

Step 1. *Always start with yourself and work backwards*.
Even if you have heard that your family is a direct descendant of George Washington, do not attempt to start there. Instead, start with yourself and work back to the earliest family member you know.

Step 2. *Write down your parents, your grandparents, great-grandparents, etc. as far back as you can go*.
Start with names, then add dates of birth, marriage, deaths, etc. as you collect the data.

Always document everything you find. Always use the women's maiden names.

Step 3. *Talk to the oldest members of your family to get as much information as you can from them.*

Ask pointed questions about their childhood, the places where they lived, what they remember about their parents and grandparents, their courtship and marriage, the birth of their children, their own homes, their pets, their jobs. If they tend to ramble occasionally, let them go. Sometimes you can miss the most delightful stories by trying to be too legalistic in your questions. If they do not object, tape record the interview to make sure you don't get wrong dates, etc. Always check these dates and names later; memory does tend to fail.

Step 4. *Trace the information you have gotten to the geographical area where the data originated from to verify it.*

Mistakes do happen. Tales that people hear all their lives become a part of the family history. Do not discredit them, but do not just swallow them whole. If you get proof of the facts, that is the time to enter it into your records as fact.

Step 5. *Put your information on a genealogical chart.*

These simple basic charts are available from a local Mormon (Latter Day Saints) Church or often at your public library. There are also some good general genealogy workbooks that contain such forms as family history charts, census forms, group sheets (for each individual family), etc. They are well worth the investment. These forms can be freely duplicated for your own use.

Step 6. *Check places other than vital records for specific data.*

If you have "missing links," turn to such secondary sources as census records, newspapers and local or regional history (especially centennial) books.

Step 7. *Gather as many pictures as you can find.*

One of the main problems with this is that many people over the years never labeled family pictures. Again, go to the older members of the family to see if you can get the names to go with the faces. Make copies of these pictures to include in your family history book.

Step 8. *Collect documents such as birth certificates, death certificates, marriage licenses, even tax records.*

Make photocopies of these documents to include as part of the text of your family history book. Such documents as immigration papers or citizenship certificates add a whole new side of the story to your finished book.

Step 9. *Get and record (either on tape or in writing) family stories.*

Some of these stories may not even be true, but include them if they are a part of what has made your family react and act as they do under certain situations. If you find that some of these stories are not true, be sure to say that in your book. These fables have lived long enough and they should now be put to sleep. However, they should not be killed. An example of this is a family who had believed for generations that they were descended from Noah Webster. When one of the women (in the early 1900's) fell in love, she was forbidden from marrying her lover. The reason? *No Webster would ever marry an illiterate man! The Websters are people whose lives revolve around the written word*. And so, the woman lived a life of spinsterhood. It was years later when a family genealogist discovered that Noah Webster had two grandsons, both who were killed in the Civil War and who never married. One complete line of the family never materialized, all because of a myth. Another example, which we mentioned in the beginning, is that many people claim to be direct descendants of George Washington. The only children George Washington had were his stepchildren, Martha's children from her first marriage.

Step 10. *Do not show the book to every living relative before you take it to print.*

If you have carefully and thoroughly done your research and documented it, there is no need to let everybody in the clan add their two cents worth. You will never write a family history that everybody agrees with. You will, however, often catch them showing it proudly to all of their friends and neighbors when they think you aren't looking. And if they argue, point to the proof inside the pages of your pride and joy and leave it at that.

Chapter 11
INSPIRED TO WRITE

Do your spiritual values dictate your life? Do you think you could impart some of that inspiration to other people through your writing? The inspirational writing markets today are far more abundant and open than ever before. After Sept. 11, 2001, millions of people turned to God, or their faith, or whatever term you wish to use. This will serve as a very bare bones guideline for how to break into this wide open market.

If you want to "break in," the best place to do it is in the magazine field. The down side of this is that the majority of religious magazines do not pay for freelance articles, other than in sending a few free samples of the magazine which contain your article.

The plus side of this is that each time you get an article published, that credit makes you a much more viable commodity when you approach a paying market. Never underestimate the power of the printed page, especially if it is your page. If you can list 50 published articles on your resumé, the editor who sees it is not going to write back to you and ask you how much you were paid for each of those articles.

Step 1. *Begin with your own denomination.*

Check out devotionals, Sunday school papers, and monthly magazines. Get some short articles published in your own local newsletter. If they don't have one, offer to do one for them.

Step 2. *Look for magazines you have a common ground with, theologically.*

Religious magazines and papers are very picky about this. If you are a Roman Catholic, you have almost no chance of getting your material into a Baptist magazine, or a Christian Scientist getting into a Methodist publication.

(1) Start with smaller publications. Such magazines as *Guideposts* get thousands of submissions every month.

(2) Don't limit yourself to strictly religious publications. Such magazines as *Redbook, Woman's Day, Family Circle, Rosie* and *Woman's World* publish inspirational stories in almost every issue.

(3) Once you have an "in" in the magazine field, contact your local newspaper, "clips" in hand, to see if they are interested in an occasional article.

Now, if your goals are higher and you want to write inspirational books, one of the hottest new markets is inspirational romance. You must, however, be very careful to know the market thoroughly. What will "sell" to one publisher will be labeled "sensuous" to another one. Who would have thought, a few years ago, that Harlequin would be publishing inspirational romances? Well, with their creation of Steeple Hill Romances, the unthinkable has happened. What will sell to Steeple Hill would be thrown out in two seconds flat by a publisher such as Barbour in their Heartsong Romances. Here are some of the guidelines that are considered pretty much acceptable by almost all inspirational markets.

(1) No explicit sex.
(2) No cursing.
(3) No out-of-wedlock intimacies.
(4) In many cases both the hero and heroine must be virgins.
(5) No alcoholic activities.
(6) The hero (or heroine) should not be an out-and-out sinner just waiting to be "redeemed" at the end of the book.
(7) The "romance" should be much stronger than the "physical attraction" or "chemistry" between the hero and heroine.

(8) Dress should be modest. Some publishers of inspirational romances even frown on a woman wearing a bathing suit in the presence of men.

As in any genre, the best way to do research is to purchase and read several books by the publisher you hope to attract. There are some inspirational romance publishers who will consider a novella for an anthology and then will move you up to a full-length book of your own. Barbour and Tyndale House both work this way.

Following is a (very partial) list of some of the publishers who are putting out inspirational publishers. Be sure to get their guidelines before you plunge into the actual writing of your book. If you find a publisher who seems genuinely interested in your proposal and query, adhere strictly to those guidelines.

Baker Books
Barbour Publishing (Heartsong Presents)
Bethany House
Harlequin Publishing (Toronto office; Steeple Hill Romances)
Harvest House
Mr. View Publishing
Multnomah Press (Palisades Romances)
Tyndale
Waterbrook
Zondervan Publishing

Chapter 12
SEASONAL HITS

Know your market. Sounds simple, right? Too often writers look at their targeted reader—by age, gender, genre, etc. But too often we forget to look at the calendar in connection with our books. The time of the year can be the best marketing tool we have.

Some holidays, of course, are overdone. Saturated to the hilt. There are probably more tools aimed at Christmas than any one single day of the year. So, we will put that aside for the time being and below you will find a list of holidays (or seasons) that are often forgotten or ignored. If your book is already written, see where it fits on the yearly calendar. If you are working on your next book, why not center it on a certain event or day? It will make it much easier to "plug into" that marketing tool.

January—New Year's Day

Concentrate on new beginnings. This works for both fiction and nonfiction. If you are writing a romance, imagine a woman whose husband has deserted her and her children (whether through divorce, death or whatever). What better way to give a person hope than to introduce hope for a new life. If you are more inclined to write mysteries, why not try your hand at the really evil guy getting his comeuppance in the most well-deserved way you can. Justice prevails! If you write nonfiction, an inspirational collection of people who suffered defeat but who overcame can offer that little push everybody needs after a bad year.

February—President's Day

There are a lot of romances, especially, aimed at Valentine's Day. So why not move away from that. What if the hero is a guy who is as honest as Abe Lincoln—but underneath it all lies a heart as sinister as—well, whoever. Make him the bad guy in a mystery—the guy everybody trusts but who can pull off the worst crimes of the era.

Or, if you lean more towards George Washington, why not try a historical novel set during the Revolutionary War?

March—St. Patrick's Day

There are a lot of books of Irish sayings, Irish castles and Irish history. But try to put a new spin on an old story. Put an Irish cop in New York City in the center of a mystery. Put an Irish washerwoman in a historical romance. Or try an Irish wolfhound as the hero in an adventure.

April—Easter

There are almost no books written about Easter unless they are religious inspirationals. Why not use the opportunity to try your hand at an inspirational romance, where the pastor finds true love on Easter. Easter, like New Year's, is a symbol of new beginnings. If you are a little warped, you might have a mystery with some guy who is running around, acting as loony as they come, either claiming to be Jesus Christ or Judas Iscariot. Be creative!

May—Mother's Day

Mother's Day is perfect for both fiction and nonfiction. How about a do-it-yourself book of simple handicraft projects for children to make for their mothers? Or a romance that gives an elderly mother a chance at a new life after losing her lifelong mate. Or if you want something different, why not do some research on the Russian May Day celebration and do a historical novel set in the midst of it? Or a mystery where the clues are left on the doorknobs of various town citizens in May Day baskets?

June—Father's Day

How about either a mystery or a romance where the father of a family who has left home

wants desperately to get back to his family, but
he is wandering around with amnesia. Or a
family saga where the children who have been
separated since early childhood all set out to
reunite and all roads lead to Daddy?

July—Independence Day
This one is perfect for a woman's fiction
book on making her own way in a "man's
world," proving that she is up for any challenge
life—and corporate America—can dish out.

August—summer vacation
August is the only month on our calendar
that does not have an official holiday. This is
the perfect time to tap into a vacation theme. It
is traditionally known as the "slowest month"
in traditional publishing. Capitalize on that by
filling the gap.

September—Labor Day or back-to-school
How about a romance with a workaholic?
Could be either a man or woman. Or how about
an older-than-average student who is returning
to college?

October—Halloween or Columbus Day
Halloween is the perfect setting for
mysteries. Another good shot at getting a lot of
good coverage for this is a children's book of
games, etc. which can be used for parties. With
so many people worried about the dangers of

the old trick-or-treat scene, this could hit the best-seller list if you put some creativity, research and fun into it.

For Columbus Day, how about a historical that sends a young woman posing as a man who stowed away on the Nina, the Pinta or the Santa Maria?

November—Thanksgiving or Veteran's Day

Thanksgiving is the holiday when more families get together than any other except Christmas. Think in terms of family. Is there a mystery in the past that has been "hush-hush" for as long as you remember? Create a mystery to solve the problem once it surfaces over the turkey and stuffing?

Recently, in talking to a bookstore manager about *Old Habits Die Hard,* the third book in my Patrick and Grace Mysteries, I told her that it had a Thanksgiving theme.

"A Thanksgiving book that isn't either a kids' book about the Pilgrims—or a turkey cookbook? You just sold me on it!"

For Veteran's Day, a good soldier-story is a sure fire winner. Everybody loves a guy in uniform. Or why not reverse it, and have the guy fall in love with the girl in uniform?

December—the winter solstice

Forget about Christmas for a minute. Imagine a couple of astronomers who just happen to get stuck in a blizzard at the same lonely cabin. They are both dead set on finding the North Star, but they won't look in the same direction!

The previous examples are by no means extensive. They are merely suggestions to tweak your imagination.

Once you have your book written and published, the real work begins. But by the means you have created, using the calendar as your best marketing tool, you have something to offer to both online and book and mortar bookstores. You have the best tool you could possibly have. You have a product that will fill a niche that has long been empty. Pitch your book to store managers far and wide. With just a little extra work, you can be the one book that will find a place on an end-cap in a bookstore, or on a front rack, or on the very top of the online store when you open their site. Make them realize that you have the best thing invented since sliced bread!

Chapter 13
RADIO INTERVIEWS

There are a lot of old wives' tales that affect our every-day life. Some of these fables have to do with our everyday life. When television first came out, people said all movie theaters would be forced to close. With the advent of computers, people said the postal system would become obsolete and paper would no more be necessary. Radio was certain to be outmoded with television. The Oscars are proof positive that the first statement was in error. More things are printed out from computers than ever. Have you ever tried to watch television while driving on a busy freeway? If in no other venue, radio is by far the most popular means of entertainment and enlightenment in automobiles than anything else. So, radio provides an excellent opportunity to air news of your book—and yourself—than ever.

The cream of the crop, radio wise, is National Public Radio. Besides, it is the most likely way to reach the "reading population" in the country. In fact, it goes far beyond just the boundaries of the United States. The NPR web site says it like this: NPR Worldwide can be heard around the world on over 140 radio stations, in over 25 million satellite homes, in 7 million cable homes, and throughout Europe, Africa and Asia on World Space, and last but not least, on shortwave everywhere. You can't get much better outreach than that.

In this PromoPak, we will give some general instructions on how to locate radio stations, how to contact them, how to make your "sales pitch" appealing and how to keep from being a boring radio guest. Beyond that, and perhaps even more importantly, you will find a list of online web sites that will provide you with numerous places where you can find listings of radio stations, state-by-state.

One final word before we dig in. The majority of radio interviews are done by telephone from your own home. This has several advantages: you are more relaxed in your own surroundings; your outreach has virtually no geographical boundaries; finally, you don't even have to get dressed up all fancy to go. I have a very good friend who used to work for a newspaper. Due to cutbacks, he was out job hunting. He tried for a couple of radio spots, but didn't land either of them. Then he tried out for a position as news director at a local television station. He said what has become one of my favorite quotes: "I have a newspaper voice and a radio face."

Okay, let's get to work.

Step 1. *Locate local radio stations.*

Local radio stations are always pleased to have "celebrities" they can feature. To do this, you can check on the web sites we list at the end of this PromoPak. Or, you can take phone directories from your own area and check in the yellow pages under "Radio stations and broadcast companies." Begin in your own back yard. This allows you to get a track record, so when you begin to branch out farther you can say, "I was the guest on..." and list the call letters of the stations you have been on, the name of the program host, and the date you appeared.

Step 2. *Talk to the host of the program on which you will appear.*

This is vital. A radio interview can be a nightmare if the personalities of the host and the guest clash. If you feel, when you speak on the phone, how the two of you communicate. If you sense tension, try to put him or her at ease. Find some common ground, even if it isn't your book. Yes, the host is a pro at this and you are a rank amateur, but you can still take the lead if it is necessary.

Step 3. *Set up the time*.

This is so basic it hardly seems worth stating. Still, the obvious is sometimes overlooked. Make sure you write the date and the hour on your calendar. You don't want to be involved in something else when the phone rings and the time arrives.

Step 4. *Go over the background of your book in your mind*.

This means not just the plot, but how you got the idea, how you actually do the writing (how long it took, what kind of writing schedule you keep, how you did the research), the path you took to get it published, how long after it was accepted by a publisher until it actually was out and available for sale, what the reaction has been.

Step 5. *Advertise*.

Inform everyone you know when and where you will be on the radio.

Step 6. *Inform the local bookstores well in advance.*

One of the questions that will *always* be asked is "Where is your book available?" Make sure the bookstores have plenty of copies of your book on hand. If possible, set up a book signing for the following day.

Step 7. *Make posters and put them up.*

These do not have to be fancy, but if you can include a picture of yourself, a picture of your book cover, the date and radio station, this can do wonders for increasing your listening audience. Where do you put them? If you live in an apartment building, put one up there. Put them in the grocery stores, the library, laundromats, mall bulletin boards, anyplace you know there are people who read the bulletin boards. One word of caution here; some of these places require you to get permission from the service desk before you post things.

Step 8. *Verify the appointment.*

Do this just one day before you are to appear. If there is a worldwide emergency, of course you will be postponed, but barring that, you want to make sure they remember that you are to be the guest on the following day.

Step 9. *Make preparations at home.*

Even though you are in your own home for the interview, make sure you have made proper arrangements in advance for such things as child care for your children, the dog and cat are well under control (and outside if possible), that the ringers on other phones are turned off, nothing is cooking on the stove and you are far enough from the doorbell that if anyone rings it the host won't be able to hear it and the "ringer" will think you are not at home.

Step 10. *Take charge if necessary.*

This usually doesn't happen, because the interviewers are pros who know how to lead a conversation, avoiding what is called "dead space," which is a period of time of silence. Above all, don't freeze! If the host asks you a question, be quick to respond. If the question brings something interesting or amusing to mind, even if you haven't covered it with the interviewer in previous conversations, by all means veer a little. An interviewer would far rather have a guest who talks too much than one who talks too little.

Step 11. *Don't overlook tie-ins.*

If the radio station is in the area where your book is set, by all means tell about the relationship between your book and the location. When you are on the radio, location is a very vital part of the plugs that will endear you to readers.

Step 12. *Stretch your wings.*

Once you have done several local or regional radio interviews, begin to reach farther out. You probably won't land a spot on Larry King Live or Oprah, but you can gain a lot of popularity by expanding your horizons. Be sure to include the places that your book addresses. If it is set on Cape Cod, contact radio stations there. If it is in San Francisco, head in that direction. If you speak a foreign language, such as Spanish or Italian, and there are radio stations with at least part of their programming in those languages, arrange for interviews there. Even though your book is in English, many people who speak other languages also read English.

Step 13. *Don't overlook all the Internet Radio stations.*

This is a fairly recent development, and it seems like there is a new one springing up almost daily. I had never done much with them, other than a couple of interviews, until one of them (Passionate Internet Voices Talk Radio, which can be found at http://internetvoicesradio.com) came knocking on my door, asking me to host my own program. I now have two weekly radio programs on there: "Marketing for Fun and Profit" and "What's Happening?" If you are interested in getting your feet wet and want to have an interview with me that is guaranteed to be fun and relaxed, e-mail me at pivtrprograms@yahoo.com. We'll get you set up.

One of the advantages of Internet radio is that most programs go onto a pod-cast and are available for quite some time after they air live. This makes it easier to promote the programs to friends and fans who missed it the first time around.

Now, you are on your own. It is time to equip yourself with a list that will direct you to the places where you can locate countless radio stations. Before you know it, you will be a famous person. Now all you have to do is get the riches to go with it. Every single book sale helps you reach that goal as well.

WEB SITES FOR LOCATING RADIO STATIONS:

www.npr.org/members
www.gebbieinc.com/radiointro.htm
www.newslink.org/stratradi.html
www.radio-locator.com/cgi-bin/page?page+states
www.radio-directory.fm/st_list.cfm
www.links.radio-online.com/stations.htm
www.topradio.com
www.live-radio.net/us.shtml
www.christianradio.com
www.allaboutjazz.com/radiostations.htm
www.radioscout.com/servlet/RadioScout.MainPage
www.carnegielibrary.org/subject/media/radio.html

Chapter 14
E-GROUPS

One of the most amazing things about writers is their willingness to share—their generosity. One of the most evident ways of doing this is through what is called "e-groups." If you do not belong to any such groups, commonly called "communities," it is time to rectify that.

If you are a member of AOL (American OnLine) or MSN (Microsoft Network), there are many such groups among their offerings. Just go to www.aol.com or www.msn.com and do a search for Writers e-groups.

If, however, you do not subscribe to either of these networks, you are still in luck. One of the biggest offerers of e-groups is found at www.yahoogroups.com . Once you get to their home page, quickly scroll down to Entertainment and Arts and click on "Books." You will find a listing (by group) as of Nov.

2007, 96053 under "Books and Writing," 15,159 under "Publishing," 35537 under "Reading groups," 3317 under "Reviews," and 7536 under "Genres."

Pick which group fits your needs most closely, then go through the list and select those which are most appealing. A couple of things to watch for are the number of members and the number of "posts" daily, or at least weekly. If there is little or no activity in the group, it is probably a waste of your time. If you are hard-pressed for time and the group you are most interested in has 40-80 posts per day, you might find yourself bogged down with the messages you receive and your e-mailbox overflowing.

Here is the simple way to join these groups, and a few tips about posting, etc.

Step 1. *Once you select a group you want to join, hit "Join this group" at the top of the page.*

Step 2. *Type in the requested information.*

Step 3. *As soon as you see that your membership has been approved, send them a message, telling a little bit about yourself.*

You should definitely tell what book or books you have written, who your publisher is and any other pertinent information about our background. This should include not only your writing, but a little about yourself personally. These people tend to bond almost like families.

Step 4. *Reply to several messages right away, especially if they are addressed to you or are to welcome you.*

This shows them that you are not there ONLY to sell your books, but to share and to learn.

Step 5. *Beware of using the group solely to air your wares.*

This is known as "BSP" (blatant self-promotion) and is strongly frowned upon. Once you are an accepted part of the community, the joys of a new acceptance or the release of your book are hailed proudly by one and all.

Step 6. *If you are overwhelmed by the number of messages you receive, go back to the homepage of the group and click on "Edit Membership."*

You can go onto "digest" or checking the messages at the home page rather than on a "Daily view" of the messages. This means that you will get "clumps" of 20-25 messages delivered in one post one or two times a day or that you can simply go to the home page, click on "Messages" and read the messages that have been sent that day without them ever entering your own mailbox.

Step 7. *Make sure you have a "signature line" at the end of each of your posts.*

This is not viewed as "BSP," but does enable you to remind them each time you send a message of your book, web site, etc. A signature line can be created at your e-mail address, usually listed under "options." Make sure you click on "Save" once you have created the signature line so it will appear on each and every message you send to anyone.

Step 8. *Participate actively in the daily posts, but try not to be argumentative*.

If you have learned something exciting, don't be afraid to share it. Sure, you might help someone else sell a couple of their books, but they in turn will do the same for you.

Step 9. *If you have to "disappear" for awhile because of a writing deadline, or you will be away from a computer for awhile, or you are moving, or whatever, be sure to let the group know before you leave*.

If you don't, when you return you will undoubtedly find a whole pile of "Whatever happened to..." posts. It is better to let them know ahead of time.

Step 10. *Some groups have strict rules and regulations about what can and cannot be posted.*

Be sure to adhere to these guidelines or you will find yourself being privately (hopefully) chastised by the moderator of the group. You may even find that you are banned. It is wise to "keep your nose clean" if you want to get all the benefits you can from the group. However, if you find that there is something offensive on the posts or that you are not benefiting from it in any way, don't be afraid to unsubscribe. There is sure to be another group you can subscribe to that will more closely meet your needs.

Step 11. *If you find that you are spending most of your time on the Internet talking to other writers and your own writing is suffering, cut back*.
At least until you have completed the project that is staring you in the face.

Like everything else in writing, have fun. It used to be true that writing was a very lonely career. Today, thanks to the Internet and e-groups, that is no longer true. It is a sharing, learning, enjoyable life.

Chapter 15
SEARCH ENGINES

Have you ever wandered around aimlessly on the Internet, trying to find the one thing you are looking for? If you have, you soon learned that with the vast amount of information available online you need help. This is where *search engines* come into play.

What is a search engine? It is a site that has been set up to conduct an online search for the information you are looking for. It is, basically, an encyclopedia of data, which can be found by subject.

What does this mean to an author? It means that if you are looking for some specific piece of information, it is just a few letters and a click away. But even more importantly, it means that if someone else is looking for information that is contained in your book, they might find your book there for their use.

How do you get onto a search engine? It is as easy as 1-2-3.

Step 1. *Go to one of the most common search engines and type your name into the search space.*

(A list will follow.)

Step 2. *If your name shows up, click on each entry to see what it has to say about you.*

You might be surprised by how much people already know about you.

Step 3. *Type in the name of your book in the search space.*

Again, click on them to see what it says.

Step 4. *If your name is not there, type the following into the search space: free search engines.*

Step 5. *Follow the instructions and register for membership.*

It is imperative that you have already followed the information on how to set up your own web site. That will be the primary thing you will want to show up if someone else is looking for you.

Step 6. *If the search engine you sign up for has links to other search engines, continue to follow through on them to sign up for as many as you can.*

Step 7. *Be sure to include "key words" that appear in your web site.*

For example, if you have written a historical romance set in Scotland, do not enter the key word of "Romance," but be more specific, as "Scottish Romance." The more exact your key words are, the more people will be apt to find your data if they do a search by subject. They may never have heard of you, but if your book is about building birdhouses they will find you by entering a search for birdhouses.

Step 8. *Do another search for search engines.*

This will bring you to those engines which charge for being listed in them. Scan through them and see if there are any that seem to cater to your subjects.

Step 9. *Find web-zines or e-zines that carry articles about your area of expertise.*

Step 10. *Locate the e-mail address for these online periodicals and contact them, offering to write an article for them.*

Many of these sites do not pay dollars and cents, but they still give a vast amount of publicity and exposure, which is invaluable to an author.

Step 11. *Once they have agreed to publish your article (and not all of them will, just as in the print-version magazines), go back and again put your name into the search engine where you first spotted the magazine.*

Your name will now appear on these additional search engines, and it didn't cost you a cent.

Step 12. *Be creative*.

Find popular or famous people to "tag onto." Author Janet Elaine Smith has a page on her web site, "John Grisham and Me." His books chronicle her life in an uncanny, almost eerie way. You can do a search on countless search engines for "John Grisham" and you will come up with Janet Elaine Smith, who is certainly not nearly as well-known as John Grisham. But if it continues, one day she just might be!

Below are the top six search engines, in the order of hits they receive weekly, as well as the number of minutes the average user spends on their site looking for information.

Search engine	No. of hits weekly	Avg. time spent
Yahoo	34,650,198	36 min.
MSN	33,029,923	29 min.
Google	10,368,261	8 min.
Lycos Network	8,301,088	8 min.
InfoSpace	3,941,684	6 min.
Ask	3,695,872	6 min.

Here's a bonus for you:

To register on 100 free Search Engines, go to http://www.submitplus.com/bestmain.htm or http://www.ineedhits.com.

Chapter 16
SHARING WHAT YOU KNOW

One of the best ways to increase your own knowledge is by teaching what you know to others. Sound backwards? Just ask any teacher and they will tell you that they are constantly learning.

In today's technological world, we have not only the option of teaching in a real physical classroom, but also can teach others how to write via the Internet. This can be done in conjunction with other on-line schools, perhaps with your publisher, or even on your own web site. Yes, it takes some promotion to build your class up—like everything else in a writer's life—but the rewards are tremendous.

Some people argue that you can't teach a person to write. Either a person is a writer or they aren't. It is an inbred ability. While this might well be basically true, the foundations of what makes a story or an article can be learned.

What makes a *good* story or a *good* article is up to the individual.

While we will touch on the elements of writing articles and writing non-fiction books, this PromoPak will deal primarily with fiction writing and how to teach its fundamental elements.

This is what you should present to your class as to how to write nonfiction for magazines, newspapers or books.

Step 1. *Choose a topic you are interested in.*

Even if you are not an expert, if it is something you would like to know more about, you can write about anything in the world as long as you are willing to do the necessary research. With the Internet, this is at the touch of your fingers and a search engine.

Step 2. *Make it interesting.*

An editor was heard to say to one of his regular writers, "In order to be competitive in today's market, we have to *dumb down* our articles." What he meant was that the article had to be on a level that appealed to all sorts of people.

Step 3. *Use verbal illustrations.*

There is no need for non-fiction to be boring. By the use of illustrations, whether from your own personal life, from history, or from observation, this can breathe life into your writing.

Step 4. *Use photographic or artistic illustrations.*

This is an option that is not available for fiction writing, unless you are writing a children's book. Think of the articles that appeal to you in a magazine, or a how-to book. It is much more enticing to have a picture of a lemon meringue pie than to simply read the ingredients.

Step 5. *Be thorough.*

Don't leave any stone unturned. If you are writing an article about home schooling, don't stop with the "how-to" aspect of it, but finish with the "what happened" points of how these students compared with the children from "traditional schools" when they entered college. If you are doing an instructional book of crochet patterns, don't just show the basic steps, but take a photo of the finished afghan or tablecloth. Remember the phrase you have heard a million times in your other classes: *show, don't tell.*

Step 6. *Always check with authorities on the subject about which you are writing.*

Nothing gives more credence to your writing than to be able to cite professional sources. Be sure to list these sources at the end of the article or at the back of the book.

This is the curriculum that has been used in a fiction writing course, taught for several years in an adult education class.

FICTION WRITING FOR BEGINNERS

Week 1. Paving the way.

Select the genre.
The best way to do this is to stop and consider what you like to read. If you love romance but hate mysteries, don't try to write a mystery just because you think it will sell better.

Choose your location.
If this is your first fiction-writing experience, it is easier to select a geographical location you are familiar with. However, if you are a good researcher and you have a specific place in mind, don't let the inability to travel there stop you. After all, fiction writing is all about creativity.

Choose your main characters.
Consider the audience you are targeting your book towards. You don't want to write about a bunch of old people if you are doing a children's book, although you can certainly include some of them in it. If you are writing for an elderly crowd, don't make all your characters in their 20's.

Decide on the time or era in which your story will be set.

Select your main plot line.

At this point, you do not have to deal with specifics. Just set up the main idea of the story. It will evolve as you begin writing.

Assignment for Week 1:

Before the next class, write a synopsis of the story, including information about the characters, the time frame, the location and the plot. Maximum of 2 pages.

Week 2. Discuss the ideas of each student's stories.

Select one person's story.

Work on it together, bouncing ideas around to begin to create the scenario of the book. Let the creativity build the "flow" of the story.

Concentrate on the setting of the book.

Discuss places to find information on the location. Good resources are travel guides, chambers of commerce, magazines (National Geographic is one of the best), Internet web sites, phone directories, history books. You can write a book without ever leaving your hometown. If you are writing about your hometown, talk to tourists. People who live in the Black Hills of South Dakota have often never seen Mount Rushmore.

Assignment for week 2:
Translate the information you have learned in class to your own book. Do an extensive written report of the important and also the seemingly insignificant points of the location you have chosen. Instruct each class member to bring a package of 3x5 file cards to the next class.

Week 3. Concentrate on the creation of your characters.

Write the name of each of your main characters on a separate card.

List their physical traits.
Hair color and length, eye color, height, weight, birthmarks, any unusual marks—big nose, limp, lisp, whatever you see when you close your eyes and envision them.

List their hobbies.

List their quirks and idiosyncrasies.
Nervous tic, curl their hair with their fingers, bite their fingernails, chain smoker, eats constantly.

List their family background.

Tell where they have lived and what their jobs are.

Do this for each of your minor characters as they appear in your books.

Assignment for week 3:

Take your 3x5 index cards and put the characteristics of your characters onto them. Use some of the information in the next chapter in your book.

<u>Week 4. Center this week on the era in which your book is set.</u>

What do you know about the time?

Did you live in the time your book is set?

What historical events occurred?

How did these events affect the lives of everyday living?

What were the fashions, the food, the entertainment, the houses, the jobs, everything that shaped the lives of people in that day?

Where can you find further information?

Old encyclopedias, history books, regional magazines (if current setting), Internet web sites.

Assignment for week 4:
    Bring some pictures to the next class of the actual setting of your book. (If it is a futuristic book, try to create a drawing of the location, according to your imagination.)

Week 5. Develop the actual story line.

Go back to the original story you worked on in Week 1.

Work together to build the main plot.

Try to fit your discussion into your own story.

Assignment for Week 5:
    Bring the first chapter, complete and edited, to the class to be read together in the class for Week 6.

Week 6. Discuss what to do with your book is completed.

Publishing options.
    Traditional publishers
    Print-on-demand publishers
    E-publishers
    Self-publishing
    Vanity publishing (not recommended)

Stress the importance of knowing the market. It is a total waste of time to send a mystery to a romance publisher or an adult science fiction book to a children's publisher. Once you settle on a publisher to whom you want to submit your manuscript, make a phone call to the main office to get the name of the appropriate editor. MAKE SURE YOU KNOW THE CORRECT SPELLING OF THEIR NAME.

When you think your manuscript is ready for submission, go over it at least three more times, looking for typos, grammatical errors, skipped lines or spaces, EVERYTHING. If you don't know the rules of common English, it is well worth the money to hire an editor to do the "polishing" of your work. Even if the publisher has editorial services, if it is full of mistakes, it will never be read, even if it is the next Great American Novel.

Assignment for week 6:

Write at least three query letters to an appropriate publishing house. Even if you don't send it out, file it away and see how appropriate it is when your book is finished.

Chapter 17
NEWSLETTERS

When Christmas rolls around each year, your mailbox quickly fills with family and friend newsletters. Many a person curses their arrival, yet the recipients do read them. After all, it is probably the only time of the year you hear from many of these people.

For an author, a newsletter is a valuable tool. It is the most economical way of keeping your readers updated on what is happening in your writing world.

We will discuss two phases of newsletters. First, we will determine how to create a mailing list. Secondly, we will address what to include in your newsletter and how to keep it from being tossed as "junk mail."

How to create a mailing list:

Step 1. *Gather a list of interested people from these locations*
　E-mails you receive
　People you know from your "normal" life
　People who post reviews of your books (i.e. on amazon.com, etc.)
　Alumni from your college or high school
　A list you collect at book signings, etc.
　Signers of the guest book on your web site

Step 2. *Accumulate your online addresses together*
　On your e-mail server (or)
　On your web site server (or)
　On your home Internet server (or)
　In a database such as Microsoft Word, Works, etc.

Step 3. *Accumulate your snail mail addresses*
　In an address book (or)
　On a database that will print out address labels

Step 4. *Be sure to keep your addresses current.*
　You can save hours of time by doing this so you don't have to go back and delete many addresses, look up the new address and insert the new address at a later time.

<u>**What to include in your newsletter:**</u>
　A reminder of who you are

News about your books

Clips from outstanding reviews of your books

Fun experiences from book signings or other public appearances

Upcoming events in calendar format, giving the locations where you will be

New books you are working on

Location of where your other writings can be found, both online and in print magazines, etc.

Contests you are running

Pictures of you, your family, your "events," if possible

When you are actually composing your newsletter, stop and think about the way you tackle your books. You want it to be interesting enough to hold the reader's attention from start to finish. The same is true with your newsletter. If it sounds like a boring old history teacher's lecture, the reader may get past the "Dear..." but they will never stick with it until the "Sincerely yours." Be as entertaining as you try to be in both your writing and in your public speaking.

Once you have completed both of the previous steps, you are ready to actually send the newsletter out. The Internet is a marvelous invention which makes sending a newsletter out so simple. There is, however, one "no-no" to avoid. Do not send your letter out to 10, 15 or 20 people who will show up on one e-mail address. Even if it takes a little longer, set your server so it will send your letter as a single post. That makes your newsletter look like you personally care about each and every reader; if you value them and want them to continue to buy your books, you truly do. If you send it "via bulk," the letter comes across as very impersonal, and many times it will end up in the "bulk mail" bin at your reader's e-mailbox and many people dump their trash regularly without ever looking at it.

Encourage your readers to let you know what they want from you. Include a short questionnaire occasionally to get their feedback. If you can't keep your readers happy, you might as well quit writing. Your fans deserve to be heard; they are what make it all worthwhile.

Chapter 18
WEB SITES

There is no one single thing that can do more to promote your books than your own web site. Once you have your web site created, be sure to include the url to refer people there so they can study it.

First of all, what is a *url?* That is the listing of the address that will direct traffic to your site. When you sign up for a web site, you will be issued a name to identify your site. This name usually consists of your own name, plus a variety of other words or symbols of the choosing of the site provider's decision. You can also go to various providers and register for a "domain name." A domain name is, basically, yourname.com. There are some *modified* free domain names. These are names which are fairly easy to remember, plus your own name and .com or .org. or .net, etc. You can go to a search engine such as google.com and do a search for "Free domain names." You will probably come up with quite a few choices. Do these work? Yes, but there are some drawbacks. These providers tend to be a bit short-lived. I previously had http://janetelainesmith/findhere.com . It was very satisfactory, until... One day, when I clicked on that url, the only thing that showed up was a notice saying "Page cannot be displayed." Yes, overnight they had disappeared. You are much more apt to get a long-lasting url (or domain name) if you buy one. They do not have to be expensive. Again, by doing a search on Google or some other search engine, you will find a whole group of them available. There is also the option of buying a domain name from your own web host, which is certainly the preferable route to go. The more you can keep your information and services consolidated, the better off you are, as you don't have to keep track of so many different user names and passwords. Always keep track of the official url which is given to you by the web host initially, as this will always get you back home when all else fails. For example, my "official" url is http://janet_elaine_smitho.tripod.com. By purchasing a "domain name" (which I did at www.godaddy.com) you can now reach me at http://www.janetelainesmith.com. It is a pain to type all of that in every time you want to refer someone to your web site, so use it as the "backup" system.

Which brings us to another issue. I highly recommend that you keep one separate disk with a database on it to keep all of your information such as user names and passwords on it. Or, use a plain old-fashioned notebook for this data. There is nothing much more frustrating than having to constantly hit the "Forgot password" key. Be sure that you also include, wherever you file this information, that you clearly identify what the user name and password are for.

http://www.janetelainesmith.com. This is the best type of url to use. If you plan to write numerous books, or put other things besides your books on your web site, make it as easy as possible for people to remember. Carolyn Howard Johnson preaches *branding*. Make your own name, as an author, a household word. (See later chapter on the subject of "branding.") Make everybody know who *you* are. If a reader doesn't know your url, this is the first thing they will try. Make sure it works.

Before you start to create your own web site, go to those of some of your favorite authors.

Pick out the things you like best on them and write them down. Do the same thing with the things you dislike about them. This will help you greatly as you work on your own site.

You can't imagine being able to do something like that yourself? Can't you just hire someone to do it for you? Of course you can, but it is apt to cost a sizable amount, and most authors aren't swimming in dough. So, there are ways to do-it-yourself which won't give you a migraine.

Step 1. *First of all, the most logical place to go for a possible web site is at your own Internet carrier.*

ATT, for example, will provide you with your own web site if that is where you have your Internet access. If your e-mail is at Yahoo! you might want to get a free website at geocities.com, which is owned and operated by Yahoo! AOL is probably the best-known carrier, but there is a problem with that. While they might have the most to offer, your site becomes inaccessible to the hundreds of thousands of Internet users who are not AOL subscribers. Almost all other groups can be easily accessed by anyone. Use what you already have at your fingertips.

Okay, let's assume that you are going to take the plunge and try it on your own. Many of the free hosts make it incredibly easy, even giving a tutorial tour of their facilities so you can experiment before you actually "sign up." Excuse my being personal here for a minute, but I am about as computer dumb as they come. Oh, yes, as the old cliché goes, I've come a long way, baby! If you would like to take a tour of my web site, please feel free to do so. You will find me at http://www.janetelainesmith.com .

At the end of this PromoPak, you will find a listing for some of the best free web site hosts. This list is by no means complete; it is merely to get you started.

One thing you should watch for is what is called "banner ads." Often, when you opt for a free host, you will find that there is a small banner at the top of your home page, telling people who is supplying your web site. This can be a definite drawback, as it irritates some people enormously, while others don't mind clicking to get rid of both banner ads and "pop ups." These pop up ads are the way these hosts make their money so they can afford to provide free web sites. A good idea is to check out the host to see if, after getting your web site well-established, you can upgrade your site to an ad-less site for just a few dollars a month. You will have to decide what you want to do about this issue once you have the initial site "live." Be sure to check to see how much storage space the host provides. You might think you don't need much space, but it is amazing how quickly your site will grow. Again, as you upgrade, you will have more space available for your use.

Step 2. *Now, let's get to the actual content of your web site. The first thing people will see is what is called a "Home page."*

You want to make it appealing, yet at the same time keep it simple. A cluttered, overloaded home page is probably the fastest turnoff for your visitors. The second issue is that of the time it takes to load your site. If you have too much information on your home page, it can take several minutes to gain access. A much better option is to break down the data on you Home page and put some of it onto a separate page. Make sure when you sign up for your web site that you have the choice of creating several pages. These will normally appear in an "Index," either at the top of side of your Home page (and each successive page) so a visitor can easily jump from one page to another, depending on what appeals to them. If you do not have the ability to create several pages, the guests will end up scrolling down endlessly to see everything you have on your site. This is extremely unsatisfactory to most viewers.

What should you include on your Home page? First of all, put something eye-appealing at the top. Most web site hosts have a variety of "Welcome signs" that will draw the reader in. It is also a good idea to have a photo of yourself and a short introduction to who you are. If people are reading your books, they want to know about the face behind the words they have enjoyed. If you feel that you want to share more data about yourself, such as your writing background, your education, your related fields of interest, etc., create a "Getting to know me" or "About the Author" page. If you want to include information about your family, however (other than a brief mention of them), create a "Family album" page for them to go to. Again, keep this page simple.

Step 3. *Be sure you have a picture of your book.*

If you have several books, put just the most recent one on the home page. It is also a good idea to make this image into a "link" so they can go somewhere directly to order it. You can list additional books on a "My Books" page, and be sure to link each of them to a selling-spot as well. If you go to amazon.com and they have to do a search, a recent survey reported that more than 60% of the people will not bother to order the book. That is a lot of sales you could lose because you don't link properly.

To find out how to go directly to your book at your preferred sales outlet, go to the place where you can order your book. Once you are at the "shopping cart" for your book, look at the address on the top bar on your screen. Be sure you copy it down exactly as it appears. One little dot or tittle can send a prospective buyer away in a flash if it doesn't work properly. Once you have it copied, create a link of the book cover to the place where they can buy it. Most web site hosts will give you a "check this link now" before you actually "publish" it on your web page. If it doesn't work, go back to the address and recheck it. Remember what your mother and teachers told you years ago? Practice makes perfect.

Step 4. *Another good item to have on your home page is a counter.*

This is often provided by your host. If not, there are others available that will let you put them on "foreign" sites. This will show you how many people are looking at your web site daily.

Also, add a guestbook. This will enable you to contact people by their email address when you have new books out, when you are running a contest, or basically when you have any information you want to share with them.

Step 5. *Don't be afraid to use graphics.*

These pictures, whether actual photographs or clipart, capture the attention of the viewer far more than just written words. Also, be sure to leave plenty of "white space." That means, don't make things look like they are crowded together. Don't choose a background and script color that make color it hard to read. Remember that some of your readers might be elderly folks who don't have 20-20 vision any more. You want your site as "user friendly" as possible.

Step 6. *You can create any number of additional pages you want to. Use your imagination.*

Don't be a copycat. If your books are steeped in historical research, for example, list some of the research sites you have found particularly helpful. It is far better, from the perspective of your viewers, to have numerous pages from which they can choose than to have fewer pages that they have to scroll down for what seems like an eternity.

Step 7. *Be sure to put a page up with links.*

Link to other authors, publications where you have articles available (both online and in print), reviews of your book, interviews, anything that will bring traffic back to you. Whenever you link a fellow author, make sure they will link back to you on their web site. If you have any other related web sites, make sure you link to them as well.

Once you have your web site all finished, be prepared for a lot more work. It is essential that you keep updating your site or people will come once or twice, but they will soon drop off. Come up with interesting ways to advertise your site in an interesting manner so people will want to return. I post a new advertising tip at my site weekly. I send the announcement that it is up to over a thousand people each time it changes. (Many of these are through various e-groups I belong to. See the Promo Pak on e-groups.) When your site is finished, get it listed on as many search engines as possible. (Discussed previously.)

The following is a very partial list of web site hosts.

Most of them offer a free site for you to get started, with the capability of upgrading to an ad-free one at a very low price. Don't be afraid to dig in. It is really a whole lot of fun. Yes, it can even be addictive.

www.freeweb sitehosting.com
www.angelfire.lycos.com
www.geocities.com
www.bravenet.com
www.freeservers.com
www.members.freewebz.com
www.staticFree.net
www.tripod.com
www.homestead.com

And one final place to check is here. This is a database of over 500 free web sites.
www.clickherefree.com

Chapter 19
INDEPENDENT BOOKSTORES:
AN ON-LINE MARKETING
EXPERIMENT

It is highly recommended that you use this experiment in conjunction with the information in Chapter 2—"Independence Day."

Step 1. *Write a very short description of your book* .
Use a "hook" for the first line that will catch the attention of someone who looks at these things every day.

Step 2. *End with the vital information*.
Title, author, ISBN, publisher, price, where available.

Step 3. *Save information to a floppy disk, a CD or your hard drive*
1. Go to <Edit> and click on <Cut>.
2. Close the file.

3. Open your Internet connection.
4. Do a search for <google.com>.
5. Enter a search for <independent bookstores>.
6. Go to the first entry, click on it, until you get to the actual web site for the first independent bookstore.
7. Go to <contact us> and get to their e-mail address.
8. Go to <Edit> on the top bar on your computer screen.
9. Click on <Paste>.
10. Send your message to the independent bookstore.
11. Hit the <Back> key on your computer until you are at the homepage for that bookstore. See if there are any <links>. If there are, go to each one of these and duplicate the above instructions from 10-13.
12. Be sure to keep a list of the name of the independent bookstore you sent the information to, as well as the date you sent it.
13. When you get to the point where there are no more <links>, go back to google.com and continue on, repeating steps 9-15.

When I did this, I sent information out on my first book, *Dunnottar*, to 1500 independent bookstores. In three months, I went back to the bookstores I had sent information to and after going through the first 700 of them, *Dunnottar* (as well as my second book, *In St. Patrick's Custody*) were on all but three of them! I figured if it had worked that well this far, the rest of it probably did, too. By the way, *In St. Patrick's Custody* was a "feature book" on many of these sites for St. Patrick's Day.

Chapter 20
BOOK SIGNINGS

You do not have to be a "big name celebrity" to think about book signings. There are several things you can do well ahead of time to pave the way for this event when your book is actually out. Even if you are a little "camera shy" about getting out in public, there are ways we will show you to overcome even that problem. You always dreamed about writing a book and having people enjoy your craftsmanship. Now, those very people want to meet the face behind the pen. So let's get the show on the road.

Step 1. *Get to know your local bookstore personnel.*

This is an absolute must. If a total stranger walks into the bookstore and says, "I want you to have me for a book signing," they will wonder who you are and where you came from. Every author should also be a voracious reader. There are several reasons for this: it shows you what to do—and what not to do—in your own book; it is the best way to keep up-to-date on current trends in the marketing industry; most importantly, it creates a rapport between you and the bookseller. If you have a proven track record with the people who will be selling your book, they will be as thrilled as you are when your book is available. Well, okay, *almost* as thrilled.

Step 2. *Scout out your sites*.

Take a pen and paper and carefully run through your book in your mind. Write down every possible related key word that has to do with the plot. For example, suppose your book is a contemporary romance set in the modeling world; write down the word *fashion*. Maybe you have a mystery which is in essence a *police procedural*. Write that down. Does your book involve the food industry, or is somebody "offed" at a bed and breakfast? Write down *restaurant* or *bed and breakfast*. If you have a non-fiction book on sports or hunting, write down *sporting goods stores*. Have you become an expert (through your research, of course) on child care? Write down *PTA's* and *day care providers*. Be creative. The best book signings are usually in venues other than bookstores. Authors signing their own books become passé in such a common location, but a grocery store will be thrilled to have a real live celebrity in their midst.

Step 3. *Approach your targeted market.*

With your list in hand, adhere to the well-known old marketing trick: "Let your fingers do the walking through the yellow pages." Once you have an approximate release date for your book, call the places that match up to the list you prepared in Step 2. Begin to set up book signings in these locations. At this point do not agree to an exact date for the signing. Tell them that you will be in touch with them as soon as you have your books in hand. There is nothing more embarrassing for an author, whether this is your first book or your fifty-first, than to have a book signing set in place and have no books to take with you. That is the fastest way to ruin any future signings with the place than any thing else on the face of the earth. There are too many variables in the equation to count your chickens before they hatch. It is far better to have the books sitting in a corner of your room for a week or two than have to clean the egg off your face from such an experience.

Step 4. *Order bookmarks, posters and postcards and any other promotion items you intend to use as "giveaways."*

If you can get these before you get your books, so much the better. If you have a place

149

set up for a signing, take them a poster ahead of time. It is easy to get the people where you will be doing your signing to do your advertising for you. Your main purpose is to sell books; their goal is to bring customers in. Get a self-set-up rubber stamp and set it to make an imprint of the time, place and date of your upcoming event on your bookmarks and postcards. (Such rubber stamp sets can be found in toy stores.) Pass these out at every opportunity.

Step 5. *Build a support group.*

Many authors, especially first-time authors, are very shy and self-conscious about going out and flaunting their wares. If this describes you, find out if there are any other authors in your area. If you don't know, go back to Step 1 and contact your local bookseller. They are the most likely people to know all the authors in the area. Contact the other authors and set a plan in motion to have a group signing. This accomplishes several things: you are much more apt to get broad media coverage if there are a number of authors involved; every author has friends and relatives who will come to the signing, thus drawing a larger crowd, which in turn draws the attention to the group and even more people gather; it offers a wide variety of books so a more diverse group of customers will respond. Sometimes these book signings are called "Meet the Author Events." By billing it this way, it often attracts a more elite crowd to come to the affair. Some restaurants will offer a free drink for everyone who comes in with the ad from the newspaper announcing such an event. You will find that this not only eliminates the problem of shyness, but it also gives a great opportunity for the authors to share ideas, problems, etc. and a marketing plan that will include all of the authors can be one of the most delightful parts of being a published author.

Step 6. *Move out of the ordinary world*.
Again, this may seem a repetition of Step 2, but it does in fact go beyond that. Check out the area for flea markets, farmers' markets, arts and craft shows, county fairs, auctions, any place where a crowd gathers. People are at these places prepared to spend money. Why shouldn't you get part of it?

Step 7. *Don't be afraid to do something out-of-the-ordinary to attract a crowd*.
When I do signings for *Dunnottar,* my Scottish historical novel, I often take a small "boom box" and play a CD of bagpipe music. One time I was even lucky enough to get a real live bagpiper, complete with his kilts, along. When I do signings of *House Call to the Past,* I dress as Maria Hallett. If people just pass you by, stand up and start to read from your book. Read from an exciting passage, which you have selected earlier. Do not read the end of the book

or some section that will give too much of the plot away. I can guarantee that soon people will be stopping to listen.

Step 8. *Set up your display table.*

When you actually get to the signing, don't take a stack of your books and plop them on the table and sit there with a pen in your hand. Make your table attention-grabbing. Use props, like you were creating a movie set. What makes your book appealing? When I do *Dunnottar*, I set up an actual photograph of Dunnottar Castle. I set a copy of the letter from the present owner (who praised the book for its accuracy) in front of the picture. I also set out the *National Geographic* magazine that had the feature article on the castle. For *House Call to the Past*, I put out pictures of the treasure from Black Sam Bellamy's ship, the *Whydah*, along with the article from the *National Geographic* magazine which tells about its recovery. I have an "author's bible," which holds reviews, interesting newspaper clippings, anything of interest which pertains to the books, and set it out on the table for people to browse through. With *My Dear Phebe*, I have copies of the actual letters from the Civil War that sparked the idea for the book.

Step 9. *Run a contest.*

Let the people who stop know that the prize will be awarded at the end of the book signing.

You cannot legally require them to buy a book, but guilt can do wonderful things! Do not make the prize an autographed copy of your book. That defeats the purpose of your being there: to sell books. If they think they have even a slim chance of winning the book, they will put off buying it. Make the prize something which pertains to the book. For *House Call to the Past*, I create a "Black Sam Bellamy basket," which consists of a basket containing a couple of fish-shaped candles and a string of "pearls," all three which can be bought at the "Dollar Store." When people ask what a "Black Sam Bellamy basket" is, of course you tell them they have to read the book to find out.

Step 10. *Make concessions to prospective customers.*

If you have someone who shows a great deal of interest in your book but says, "I just can't afford it until pay day," if you sense that they are really serious about it, let them know that most bookstores will hold their book for a week (some more, some less) and that you can autograph it, even though you can not make the autograph personal.

Step 11. *Have a small book or tablet there for people to sign.*

The store will usually not allow you to get the names of contest entrants or customers who bought your book, but there is nothing to stop

JANET ELAINE SMITH

you from asking the people there—whether they buy a book or not—if they would like to leave their name, address and e-mail address so you can notify them when your next book comes out. This makes the very best mailing list you can get.

Step 12. *Do individual book signings*.

One of the most fun things to do with your book is to stand in the section of the bookstores that house your book. When someone comes along and begins to look for a book in the same genre as yours, wait and let them browse for a few minutes. When they seem undecided, ask them—politely, of course—what type of book they like to read. If it is in the mystery section, rather than wait for them to elaborate, suggest the same type as yours. For example, my book *In St. Patrick's Custody* is considered a "cozy" mystery. Your book is a romance novel? Is it a historical, time travel, or contemporary? Reach onto the shelf and select your book, then ask them, "Have you read this one? It is a very good cozy mystery." (Or whatever fits with your book.) Usually they will ask you if you have read it, or just heard about it. That is your chance to reply, "I have not only read it, I wrote it." Then casually flip the copy of the book that you are holding onto the back so they can see your picture there. Then suggest that if they would like, you would be glad to autograph it for them once they get to the cash register with it.

154

Recently I was in BDaltons and did this. The woman I was talking to said, "Can you wait here just a minute?" She soon reappeared with the woman with whom she was shopping. "This is the author!" she said excitedly. The other woman said, "Well, I really prefer contemporary romances to historicals." The first woman asked, "You don't by any chance write those too, do you?" I was as pleased as punch to be able to take her around the corner to the next section and hand her a copy of *A Christmas Dream*. This was not the holiday season by a long stretch, but she looked at the book, shrugged her shoulders and said, "Oh, what the heck! I might as well get started early." By the time we got to the counter, they had each selected all seven of the books I had out. The second woman smiled as I signed her books—each one to a different person—and said, "Hey, this is great! I got half of my Christmas shopping done in the middle of the summer. And I got a Christmas book besides." The first woman jabbed her in the ribs and said, with a huge smirk on her face, "And you have plenty of time to read them yourself before you have to wrap them up."

Step 13. *Above all, have fun!*

People who pass by, even if they don't stop, will make comments about how much they admire you. If people consistently pass by, don't be afraid to stand up and shout. Well, not literally, of course, but as people turn to look but try to ignore you, make some comment like, "It's a really good book; I used to be prejudiced, but now I'm not. Other people say the same thing." Or try something like, "What kind of book do you like to read?" Or if it is near Christmas (or even if it isn't), suggest, "This book would make a great gift for your..." and then insert whatever seems appropriate, as "wife, husband, child, parents, friend," or whomever.

Chapter 21
READINGS AND LECTURES

How do you capture an audience? Well, there are a few simple rules to follow. However, the first trick is to *get* an audience to captivate. Here are some suggestions for places to find groups who are interested in both you (as an author) and your book. Call such groups or places to volunteer your services. I know some authors who charge megabucks to lecture at such places, but as a beginning author, if you make your services available for free, you will find the people in charge much more willing to cooperate and even publicize the event well in advance.

Libraries (public, private and school)
School classrooms (elementary, high school or college level)
Civic groups
Church groups

Reading groups
Senior citizen centers
Retirement homes
Stores (especially small, out-of-the-way businesses)
Coffee houses
Office supply businesses

As mentioned, this is just a very partial list, just enough to get your wheels turning. When you go into a place of business, set your book on the counter while you write out your check. See if anybody picks it up or attempts to look (usually secretly) at it. If they do, launch into your little speech about how "It will fit in perfectly with your business. Would you be interested in having me come for a book signing?" (Which can also include a reading.)

When should you do a reading?

At a book signing.
Don't wait for people to come to you. Create an interest when people are ignoring you. Don't be afraid to stand up and begin reading in the most exciting place you can find. When an audience has congregated, be sure to stop at a "cliffhanger" place in the story.

At the end of a lecture.
You are no doubt there to educate and instruct. But, don't miss the opportunity at the

end to give a sampling from your book. These people are already interested in what you have said; make the most of it.

Coffeehouses are perfect.
Even if you don't have a formal reading or signing scheduled, many such places welcome poets, musicians and writers to share their arts. Don't be shy.

Retirement homes.
The people love to have anybody come and entertain them. Many of these elderly people can no longer read by themselves. You may not sell any books, but you can be the most talked-about person in town if you will donate even half an hour a week to go read from your book. Yes, this is a chance to read it for the same group from cover to cover. And they do often buy gifts for children and grandchildren. If they can send one of your books, especially if you will autograph it, they will talk up a storm about their "famous friend." Remember, this is also a good place to take books with you to sell, as many of them find it very difficult to get out shopping. You can solve all their Christmas shopping in one trip.

How do you know what to read?

Go through your book ahead of time and select the most exciting passages.

Choose the selections according to your audience.

If you are reading to a group of children, make sure your book is appropriate.

If you are reading to senior citizens, even if you have a children's book, select the passages where there is interaction between a child and a grandparent, for example.

If you are reading to men, pick a portion that has a lot of action or intrigue in it.

If you are reading to women, pick a spot that has some romance.

If you are reading to a "general" mixed audience, aim for something mysterious.

Make sure you end on a note that leaves them begging to know "what happened."

If you finish with the end of the story, no one will bother to buy the book.

Before you go to the meeting, read through the passages several times in advance.

Make sure you are familiar with the words, the "beat" or "rhythm" of the piece. Nothing is more of a turn-off than an author who doesn't seem at home with their own works. Remember, it has been months, and in some cases even years, since you wrote the book. You want to be comfortable with it.

A good bet is to always choose a place that has a considerable amount of dialect in it.

As you read your characters talking to one another, try to remember how their voices sounded in your head when you were writing them. Don't try to imitate a Scottish or French accent if you can't do it, however. A "bad reading" is almost worse than no reading. If you are good with accents, don't be afraid to use them. It does add a lot to the presentation.

What is the difference between a reading and a lecture?

A "reading" is exactly that: various passages from your book. A "lecture" is in a more formal setting, such as a classroom, where they want to know not only about your specific book, but also about how you wrote it, how you got it published, how it is selling, the whole publishing game from start to finish.

What do I do to prepare for a lecture?

It is advisable to make some notes to follow if you are going to be giving a lecture. A good lecture should include:

(1) How you got the idea for your story.
(2) How you did your research.
(3) What kind of a schedule do you follow?
(4) How long did it take you to write your book?
(5) How did you find a publisher?

(6) Do you have an agent? If so, what is the advantage or disadvantage?

(7) How do you get your book to sell?

(8) Are you working on a new book?

(9) What is the hardest part and the easiest part of writing?

(10) Does your family support you (emotionally) in your writing efforts?

(11) Do you have another job, or are you a full-time writer?

(12) If you could never write another word, how would it affect you?

Always end with a question/answer session.

Don't be intimidated by your audience. I have heard authors who didn't graduate from high school who have lectured very successfully in colleges. Show them you are confident, even if your knees are knocking behind the podium. Remember, you have written a book and it has been published. You have done more than they have done.

Chapter 22
THE BIG CHAIN BOOKSTORES

Use this in conjunction with Chapter 1—"My Dream..."

By way of introduction.

One of the biggest complaints by authors, especially Print-on-demand authors, is, *I can't get my books into the big bookstores like Barnes & Noble, BDaltons and Borders. What can I do?*

The first thing you have to do is adopt the philosophy that nothing is impossible.

After all, stop and think about it. You have written a book; you have gotten it published. See? You have proven that you can do what millions of other people have never been able to do. Getting it into the bookstores has to be relatively easy.

In order to achieve success in this arena, you have to have a *plan of attack*. People who plan a war sit and formulate the best way to fool the enemy. Many authors consider these "big-time players" as the enemy. Okay, then let's deal with them on that level. You don't like war? Then let's shift gears and put it in another scenario. Rev. Robert Schuller, well-known television minister, spouts his "possibility thinking" gospel to people around the globe. For many years he had a special guest, whom he openly and admiringly called his mentor: Rev. Norman Vincent Peale. I jokingly told Rev. Schuller once, "When you grow up, maybe you will graduate from a *possibility to a positive force.*" You have graduated from being a writer to being a published author. It is time to get you out there in every bookstore you can find all across the country. This PromoPak will give you the 1-2-3's of how to do that.

Step 1. *Get out your Christmas card mailing list*.
These are the people you contact once a year. It is time to send them a special greeting, even if it's March or September.

Step 2. *On the following pages, enter the names and addresses of everybody you know*.
Use your Christmas card list and all other acquaintances. If you have met other authors,

be sure to include them. Nobody understands the pride a new author feels better than a fellow author. Calculate the number of people on your mailing list.

Step 3. *Buy an inexpensive greeting card software program and install it on your computer.*

Step 4. *Choose a "cute" birth-of-a-baby card*.

List your book as the baby. Print as many cards as you have on your mailing list.

Step 5. *Write a short newsletter, giving a little background about your experience writing the book.*

Then, in a fun-loving way, announce, "Please do not send gifts for the baby. Instead, go to your local big-chain bookstore and ask them to order my book. If you are very generous the day you go, ask them to order a few extra copies, assuring them that you will be telling your friends about the book and they will surely want to buy a copy of their own."

Step 6. *Include a bookmark, so they can actually see what the book looks like*.

This will have the title of the book, the author's name and the ISBN, so it will be easy for them to hand it to the bookstore clerk and get them to order it.

Step 7. *Now, begin to assemble a list of your on-line friends.*

These should include not only your personal friends, but the people who are members of your writing e-groups, bulletin board acquaintances, anyone who has been sharing your writing experiences—both the ups and the downs. Make an "on-line address book" on your favorite site, either on your e-mail carrier or your web-site carrier.

Step 8. *Go to a web site that offers "cyber greeting cards."*

(A list of some such sites will follow the steps in this PromoPak.)

Step 9. *Select an appropriate greeting card to again announce the birth of your "baby"—your book.*

Make a note of the url that will go directly to the card you have chosen.

Step 10. *Go to the word processing program you use, such as WordPerfect, Microsoft Word, etc. Write a brief note to your "cyber friends."*

List the url for the card you are sending them. Ask them, like you did on your other mailing list, to go to their local "big boy" bookstore and order your book. Be sure to include the link to your web site as well, so they can see all about the book. Make sure the book is right on the home page when they open up your web site.

Step 11. *Take a map of the United States and put a red "X" on each town you have targeted.*

This is difficult with your cyber friends, but you might ask them to e-mail you privately and let you know where they ordered the book so you can track your sales.

The above steps will not only get one copy of your book sold in each of the bookstores the people go to to order your book. I have spoken to many bookstore managers and what happens if you follow this process is absolutely amazing. Once a bookstore gets a book in, even if it a special-order for one single customer, the only way they can collect the money for the sale is to enter the ISBN number in the computer. Thank heavens for computers! The computer will see that a book by that ISBN number and title has been sold and that it is now "out-of-stock." The computer then automatically reorders the book. When that copy is sold, the wonderful computer will again reorder the book. Once the computer sees that the book is selling on a fairly regular basis, it will begin to order larger quantities of your book. The computer also sends monthly reports to the regional and district offices of the sales from each bookstore. Before too long, the district manager will begin to notice that one particular store is selling your book on a regular basis. The assumption is that it must be a good book, so they will begin to get the other stores in the district to place orders for the same book—*your book*! Before long, your book will be in bookstores all across the country. Yes, the "big boys" will still say, "We don't stock POD books." And you can just sit there and grin, as people walk in and see your book there—right alongside all the other books they regularly carry. Does this really work? You bet it does! My books are right between Bertrice Small's and Danielle Steele's all over the U.S.A.!

ON-LINE FREE GREETING CARDS:

www.bluemountain.com
www.americangreetings.com
www.cardblast.com
www.OwlGreetings.ca
http://cards.crossdaily.com (Christian)
www.marlo.com/card.htm
www.gogreet.com
www.hopesworld.com
www.akpcsales.com

This is just a beginning. If you go to a search engine like www.google.com you will find dozens and dozens more. Get to work, but above all *have fun*!

This will just give you an idea of how you can personalize this system. On www.hopesworld.com I found an antique-looking birthday card that quotes the poem that begins "Monday's child is fair of face..." Hey, my newest book is based on that poem! The title of the book is "Monday Knight"! The recipient of the card can even put in the date of their birth (date, month and year) and it will tell them, in the matter of a few seconds, the day of the week they were born. I can hardly wait to send that card to hundreds of people!

Chapter 23
ON-SITE PROMOTION

There is an old adage, but it is oh, so true. Nobody can sell a book like the author. But, how do you go about doing that? Do you have to have formal book signings? The answer is a loud NO!

One of the first rules of the game is that you should never leave home without at least one copy of your book. (Preferably two.) If you are a woman, most purses today are big enough to hold a copy of your book. If you are a man, put it in your briefcase. If you don't have a briefcase, get one. A recent survey showed that people are 78% more apt to trust a man who carries a briefcase than a man who doesn't.

Once you are "armed," what do you do with it? If you've got it, flaunt it! The people who accompany you on a regular basis may object, but they will soon mellow when they see the reaction of the people you approach.

These are not died-in-the-wool rules, but are merely suggestions. You will no doubt find many more as you get used to advertising your wares. Even though you may not be a best-selling author yet, but you are one step ahead of the majority of the people you are talking to: they have never written a book and you have.

If you are at a restaurant and there is an extra place on the table where nobody is sitting, set your book on the table for the server to see. If they don't pay any attention to it, turn it over so the back is facing upwards. They are much more apt to spot your picture on it and then the fun begins. If that still doesn't work, a simple, "Have you seen my latest fun project?" will prompt many an "Oooh" and "Aaaah." Not only will they look at it, ask about it, but before long you are apt to be questioned by a number of the other servers. Not only is this great for book publicity, but it creates a perfect opportunity to talk to the manager about having a future book signing there.

If you go into a bank or a store to cash a check, when they ask for picture ID, instead of showing them your driver's license pull out your book and show it to them. If they say they need a number, suggest they take down the ISBN. They may still insist on seeing the driver's license, but you have created a lot more interest in your book. Again, these stores are good places to ask about putting your books up for sale, especially if it is a privately owned store. (Big chains have corporate hoops to jump through to get your books in there.).

When you go into your local bookstores, where your books should be stocked by now, go to the section where your books are located. Linger in the aisle for a few minutes to watch shoppers peruse the shelves to try to make a selection. When they seem undecided, take your book off the shelf and suggest it as a good book. Most times they will ask you if you have read the book, at which point you can say "I not only read it; I wrote it." Then offer to autograph it for them if they decide to buy it.

Along with your book, make sure you always have a small supply of bookmarks with you. If the person says, for example, "I will pick it up later. Where can I buy it?" You can hand them a bookmark so when they do go to the bookstore to get it, they don't have to say to the clerk, "It was by some woman (or man) I met, but I don't know her name and I can't remember the name of the book." Instead, they will have the bookmark which should have the name of the book, the name of the author and the ISBN. If you autograph the bookmark, not only will it serve for identification for their purchase, but they will treasure it long after they have finished reading the book.

Now this may be a slight variation, but apply the same principles to phone conversations. Of course you will tell every friend and relative you know that your book is available. But let's stretch that concept a bit farther. You know how those telephone solicitors annoy you no end? Well, it is time to turn the tables. When they start giving you their little speech, interrupt them (or if they are so annoying that you can't, wait until they are done and ask for your answer). Then say something like "Since you are interested in good products, may I make a suggestion?" Then tell them about your book. Ask them if they are in front of their computer. (They almost always are, so they can click in a "Yes" or "No" for your response.) When they say they are, ask them if they can get onto amazon.com books. Everybody knows how to get to amazon.com. Tell them to do a search for either the title of the book or for your name. As soon as they say "Wow! There it is!" suggest that they place their order. Most times they will hang up, forgetting that they called to sell you something in the first place.

If you have to call to check on an order you have placed, or if you are having trouble with your phone service or your Internet server or the utility company, tell them about your book and where they can order it.

When you get a bill from someone, most of them any more have inserts or fliers advertising all sorts of things—most of them totally unrelated to the bill itself. When you return your payment, be sure to include a bookmark or a business card with your book on it along with your check. This will probably get no farther than the secretary, but secretaries probably read more books than executives do.

Don't be shy. You will be hailed as a celebrity. You can sell your book—any place and any time. But if you never tell anyone about it, it will soon die a natural death. And nobody likes a dead book.

Chapter 24
VIRTUAL BOOK TOURS

Many authors go on a "book tour." They travel from city to city, state to state, holding book signings at various bookstores. Often, large publishing houses require their authors to do these tours; it might even be part of their contract. It is not uncommon for the expenses of such tours to be paid for from the author's advance, thus it ends up costing them money, not making more money for them.

The real truth is that these book signings are unpredictable, at best. The long lines of fans that wrap around the block belong to the select few of the industry. An author who might be fairly well known might only draw a couple dozen people to the event. A lot of it depends on the advertising the store puts into it, as well as the notoriety of the author.

Many authors, especially those who are just starting out, have several problems when it comes to taking such tours. Some of the reasons why an author can't make tours include demands of their job, family obligations, schooling, disabilities, lack of funds, having to be a caregiver for another family member, as well as others.

Is there a solution? Can you still get your book out in the public eye without globe-trotting?

Thanks to the Internet, you can now take a book tour without ever leaving home.

Blogging is one of the newest crazes on the Internet. If you aren't blogging, please go sign up at one of the free ones where you can talk to your heart's content about anything you want to. You can find them by going to www.google.com and searching for "free blogs."

Once you have a blog of your own, you are ready to embark on your virtual book tour, where you will travel from one person's blog to another.

We will now embark on a "virtual book tour." All aboard! Follow our simple steps and you can be found all over the Internet, and it won't cost you a cent. (Note: there are quite a few publicists who will set up a virtual book tour for you for anywhere from $100 to $3,000. By following these steps, you can do it free.)

Step 1. *Set up your own blog.*

Readers love to get to know their favorite authors. Include "the rest of the story," telling what prompted you to write your book. Give some personal stories about yourself, your writing, your family, readers' reactions to the book, even some thought-provoking topics of discussion. On a blog, everything is fair game.

Step 2. *Advertise your blog.*

Like a good website, a blog must be publicized to be of any value. When you update your blog (which you should do at the very least once a week), let all of your friends and your fellow list-mates from the e-groups you belong to know that you have added a new post.

Step 3. *Visit other blogs regularly.*

One of the purposes of blogs is to create comments. That is the best way to know that other people are following your blog. If the visitor leaves the link to their blog, return the favor by going to see what they have to say and leave a comment for them. This can develop into a very good online friendship that can prove very useful in a virtual book tour.

Step 4. *Seek out like-minded blogs.*

Go to http://www.blogsearch.google.com and do a search by topic for things that have some connection to your book. Again, visit those blogs and comment on their entries, forming another friendship. Drop some hints from time to time about your own book. Don't try to hog the conversation; this is their blog. You don't want to offend them.

Step 5. *Make your pitch.*

Contact the owner of the blogs you have selected personally. Do not make your request publicly on their blog. Explain to them that you are planning a virtual book tour and ask if they would be willing to host you one certain day. Offer to send them a pdf of your book, thus providing an opportunity to get something out of the tour for themselves as well as helping you get the word of your book out. You can also ask for interested hosts on the e-groups you belong to. These people are already your "friends."

Step 6. *Explain how it works to the blog owners.*

You will want them to read your book, check out your website, then formulate some questions. Your blog tour will take on the format of an interview, like you were appearing on a local TV program, except that on a blog, it has the capacity of reaching around the world. Ask the hosts to send you their interview questions ahead of time so they can post them on the day they have agreed to have your "book signing." A bonus is that sometimes the host will do a book review and post it on their blog on the same day.

Step 7. *Now it's time to advertise your virtual book tour.*

It has been said several times before, but it can't be emphasized too much: nothing has any value in your virtual book tour if nobody knows it's there. Tell everybody on your mailing list to check your website daily, where you will have the various blogs listed for your fans to link to. Announce it on your e-groups. Tell your face-to-face friends and contacts. Let your publisher know about it so they can help you advertise it by putting it up on their website. Also, make sure that each day's "signing" has a link to the previous day's and the next day's blog where you will be pulling in to a whistle-stop.

Step 8. *Remember your manners.*

After you have completed your virtual book tour, make sure you thank each of your hosts. Also, let them know that if they have a similar tour themselves, you will be glad to return the favor and will host them one day on your blog.

Bon voyage!

Chapter 25
BREATHING LIFE INTO YOUR CHARACTERS

Most fiction writers get to know their characters so well that they feel they are living, breathing entities. They spend hours, days, weeks, months, and in some cases entire years with these people wandering around inside their heads. That isn't a bad thing, even though to "normal" people (i.e. non-writers) that makes authors weird.

The problem comes, though, in trying to make these people seem as real to the readers as they are to the authors. It is a writer's dream to have people relate to their characters in such a way that they can envision going on their excursions with them.

For me, the first time this happened was with Patrick O'Malley and Grace Johnson, the senior sleuths from my Patrick and Grace

Mysteries. One day when I went to church, an elderly lady came over to me and asked, "Why did you pattern Grace after me?" I told her that Grace was not really anybody, but she was a little bit of everybody. Before long, I had people telling me that they felt cheated because they wanted to have coffee with Grace every morning, instead of Anne Douglas (another character from the book) getting to sit with Grace. In the series, Patrick and Grace live in New York City, but each alternate book takes them to various places. I hear from readers every week who want to know when they are coming to their town.

The same thing happened with Monday Knight, the main character from my Women of the Week Series. Before long, readers were taking them on vacations with them to watch the planets line up from a mountaintop in Connecticut. Others were sending her on trips up the Amazon River. She gets her own e-mail, has gotten free samples of pantyhose by snail mail, and has collected more free hours of AOL and Earthlink than I have. She has gone on tour with the pop rock music group Smash and they took her along with them when they appeared on "Live With Regis and Kathy Lee."

Personally, I have had a lot of fun with my "real" imaginary people. I have created their own websites for them. I have challenged other writers to try to do similar things with their characters.

And then one day the light bulb apparently went off for somebody else. My husband is a huge fan of Law and Order, including the reruns that show over and over again on USA-TV. As I sat at my computer working on things, my back to the TV, I kept hearing over and over again two simple words: Characters welcome.

Finally, my curiosity got the best of me and I went to Google to see what it was all about. I soon learned that USA-TV had established "Characters welcome" as a branding vehicle to get people acquainted with the people from their TV programs. They set up a website for Characters welcome.

I quickly went to the website and discovered that anybody who wanted to could enter their own characters. I added one listing for Patrick and Grace and another one for Monday Knight. One of the questions it asked was if there was a url that would point the people who were going to check out the characters on the Characters Welcome website.

That's when the idea hit me. There were very few of the characters I looked at that had their own website. I decided to capitalize on the idea and set up my own business at http:// characters-welcome-websites.tripod.com . I offered to do reasonably priced websites for authors to help them bring their characters to life for their readers and fans.

Here are a few easy steps to follow to bring your characters to life.

Step 1. *Get your characters in the limelight locally.*

If you have a book signing or reading, pretend that you *are* your character. Make people believe they have really met them.

Step 2. *Alert the media to the character's events.*

You can do this in the arts department of the local newspaper, on a radio or TV interview, or as a human-interest story. If there is a local/regional magazine, approach them with the idea of introducing your character to them.

Step 3. *Ask a local celebrity to help you promote your characters.*

Is there a local band that is having a concert? What about a play or a theater presentation? They already are pretending to be somebody else, so why not let them take it one step farther?

Step 4. *Watch for things in the news that you can tie in to with your character.*

My time travel *Par for the Course* has a woman golf pro. Shortly after it was released, the CBS program *60 Minutes* ran a commercial asking one simple question: "Is a woman golf pro par for the course in the future?" I raced to send press releases all over, using the headline, "Character from Janet Elaine Smith's latest novel, *Par for the Course*, hits CBS's *60 Minutes*—almost."

Step 5. *Give your characters a cause.*

Patrick and Grace have become advocates for the homeless. Monday Knight has taken on drunk drivers. The Keith clan (from the Keith Trilogy) has fictional characters who are so real to members of the family that they have held a wake for "the Keiths who never really lived—because they should have!"

Step 6. *When you do an interview with an online group, instead of answering the questions as the author, give the responses like they were coming from your character.*

You might check on Google (or your favorite search engine) to see if you can find some samples you can look at.

Step 7. *Make a website for your character.*

For a couple of samples, go to http://crumbycapers.tripod.com or http://meetmondayknight.tripod.com.

Step 8. *Set up a blog for your characters.*

Invite readers to ask them what they think about different issues, or why they acted or reacted the way they did in the book.

Step 9. *Above all, have fun with your characters.*

If they are real to you, you can make them real to your fans too. Before long, they will be asking for "More! More! Encore!" And then, you will have the beginnings of a whole new series. And the more they know and love your characters, the more you will be in demand. It is a good thing to be "Wanted," as long as it isn't with your picture hanging on the wall in the post office!

Chapter 26
ON THE ROAD AGAIN—VIDEO TRAILERS

For some reason, when I think of a video trailer, my mind flashes to an old movie that starred the late Lucille Ball. I don't remember the name of the movie, but there was a scene where they were on a mountain road and were pulling a travel trailer. The trailer came loose from the car and it went careening down the road, ahead of the car.

Now we have video trailers for everything from music to political campaigns to sex and even your weekly sermon. Yes, and there are plenty of video trailers for books. It seems to be the hottest new fad in the cyber world.

I have several video trailers myself, thanks to a very good friend, Billie A. Williams. You can find them listed on my website at http://www.janetelainesmith.com on the home page.

You can, of course, hire somebody to make a video trailer for you, or you can get brave and tackle it yourself. I'm told it isn't really that hard. Since I have never done one myself, I won't try to give detailed information on how-to, but I have picked up some bare bones beginning information that might help you, should you decide to take the plunge.

Kristie Leigh Maguire, founder of Star Publish LLC, has made a couple of knock-out videos for her books. Some of the following information came from her, with my thanks.

Step 1. *If you have Windows XP, you can go to "Start" when you first open your computer. Go to "Programs" and locate Microsoft Windows Movie Maker*.
You will find some pretty basic hints on how to make your own movie or video trailer.

Step 2. *Study existing video trailers.*
What exactly is a video trailer? Have you been to a movie lately? If so, you will have seen a smattering of upcoming attractions. Even on TV, there are modified upcoming programs at the end of almost every one. These are, in effect, video trailers.

The best way to see what video trailers are like is to go to someplace like YouTube.com and study a whole array of them. Write down the things you like, as well as the things you don't like. Listen to the music on the videos. Does it match what you are seeing on the screen?

Step 3. *Collect your materials.*

Before you actually start the process of creating your video trailer, collect a good variety of pictures you want to use. Use as many of your own pictures as possible. If you want to use pictures that are posted on the Internet, make sure they are either royalty-free pictures or that you get permission from the owner of the pictures. The last thing you want is a lawsuit for copyright infringement.

Step 4. *Once you have your pictures assembled, decide what sort of audio you want on your trailer.*

Do you want a narration that tells the background and pitch line of the book? You can also run words on your video, which may duplicate your narration. There is no point in simply reading what is written on the screen. Many videos use music along with the written words and pictures. Again, make sure you aren't "pirating" the music you use.

Another option for music is if you know somebody who is talented and who is looking for exposure for their music, you might strike up a deal where you will give them some free publicity by listing the credit for the music in exchange for them letting you use their music. They might even compose something specifically for you and your book. Ed Teja is one musician who will do this for a nominal cost.

Step 5. *Find your market place.*

Once you have the video constructed to your satisfaction, what do you do with it? There are a lot of places where you can upload your video trailer where people can easily access it. Most of these sites are free. Here are just a few of them.

YouTube (the most popular one)
Yahoo Videos
AOL Videos
YouAreTV
Dailymotion
Revver.com
Grouper.com (Christian content only)
GodTube (Christian content only)

Step 6. *Spread the word.*

Write up a press release (see that section in the PromoPaks). Add the url of where it can be found on the signature line on your e-mails. Put the link of where to see it up on your website, in a prominent spot. Tell your friends. Advertise it on the e-groups you belong to. If you do interviews on the radio, TV, e-zines, newspapers, etc., make sure you mention it and let them know where they can find it on the Internet.

You are probably not ever going to be as famous as Lucille Ball, and you won't make the big screen with your video trailer like she did with her trailer, but do your dead level best to

192

make your video trailer the best it can be and hopefully people will remember it as long as I remember that silly movie!

If you are like me and not brave enough to try your hand at making your own video trailer but you still want to get in on the latest craze, you can contact either Billie Williams at billie@billiewilliams.com or Kristie Leigh Maguire at kristieleighmaguire@yahoo.com and if you tell them you saw their name in Janet Elaine Smith's PromoPaks, I promise they will give you a good deal. At least I know they won't "up" the price because of it!

Chapter 27
MOOOOOOVE OVER; IT'S BRANDING TIME!

Any cowpuncher can tell you that when it comes to branding his cattle, you have to strike while the iron is hot. The same is true of your "brand" when it comes to your books.

What is a brand? A brand is simply the image or icon that will identify your product as soon as someone sees it. Think about the "golden arches." Your mind instantly goes to a McDonald's. Many years ago Proctor and Gambles was labeled as Communist by many people because of their logo. (Fortunately for them, that phase passed and they are now considered a very legitimate company.) Television jingles are another way of branding a product. When you hear, "I am stuck on..." you know what it is that is stuck on you before you hear the words "Band-Aid."

You want to do the same thing with your writing. Most authors anymore want to be more than the one-book-wonder Margaret Mitchell. Her name is emblazoned in history for *Gone with the Wind*. However, if you plan to make writing a career, you want people to remember your name, not just the title of one of your books.

As we have discussed in many areas of your promotional efforts, it is once again time to put on your creative beanie and get your mind whizzing on new ideas. Don't get stuck in a rut. There are already tons of brands out there for your well-known fellow authors. Mary Higgins Clark is known as "The Queen of Mystery." John Grisham could perhaps be called "The Legal Beagle." Stephen King, "The King of Horror." Even some of the lesser-known independent authors have come up with their own brands. Carolyn Howard-Johnson has "Frugal..." written all over her face, even though she has also written both fiction and poetry. It is up to you to come up with something just as catchy, but that sets you apart from other writers.

First of all, examine the type of books you write. If you write in strictly one genre, that is relatively easy. Romance? What about "Finding Love in All the Wrong Places." Time-travels? Maybe something like "History—with a twist." Science fiction? Try "Entering new labs." Dark, evil horror? "Usurping the Ugly."

I know. I tend to get carried away. That is not meant as your motto, but it will hopefully spark some out-of-the-ordinary phrases for you.

But what happens if you write in different genres? That was the dilemma I faced in trying to brand myself. As I thought about it, trying to figure out something that would cross the lines I had crossed, I lamented, *I don't follow any one single path. I go on so many different roads.*

Aha! Inspiration hit. I came up with, "Explore roads less traveled in a Janet Elaine Smith Novel."

The next step is to figure out what to do to publicize your brand. I have a favorite "haunt" online. It is found at http://www.vistaprint.com . They have more promotional materials available than you can imagine, and more than you could possibly ever use. One of the big bonuses is that after you place your first order there, they will send you "free" offers almost every week. These can be for everything from 250 free business cards (their basic business cards are always free, but you often get a free offer for their more streamlined cards which you can personalize with added images, etc.), 25 free brochures, 25 free flyers, 100 free standard sized postcards, 50 free over-sized postcards, free magnets, free note cards, and much more. Their quality is the best I've ever seen. If you get the free offers, you have to pay the shipping and setup fee, but it is still minimal.

I began to peruse VistaPrint's site for roads. I searched for "mountain roads," "rural roads," "roads in forests," "bike trails," and more. I found some of the most beautiful roads you can imagine! I went to work, making all sorts of fun things that I could hand out to people I met, could send to bookstores that carried my books, to friends I sent birthday cards to... Well, you get the picture. And on every one of them, I used the phrase I had chosen for my brand: "Explore roads less traveled in a Janet Elaine Smith Novel."

Before long, I began hearing from people who had seen my branding materials. I would often get comments like, "I decided to explore your road, and I liked the place it took me."

The next step, after making up the promotional items, was to get it up on my websites. I did a search for "free banners" and the one I found that worked the best was at www.BannerGenerator.org. They have hundreds of images to choose from, and finding roads, paths, trails, etc. was easy. The hard part was in choosing which ones I liked best. Once I had that settled (actually, I made several different ones as long as I was there, and I simply saved them to my hard drive so I could vary them), I put a banner at the top of my websites. You can see them at either http://www.janetelainesmith.com or http://janetesmithstarbooks.tripod.com. (I say that not to boast, but to provide you with an example.) Then I invited anyone who stopped by my websites to help themselves and place them on their websites as well. (This is called a "banner exchange," and it is a great way for authors to cross-promote one another.)

If you have letterhead made up, use your "brand" on it. Use it on your e-mail signature line. Use it on all of your printed material. Use it in your bio at the end of articles you write. Use it when you talk to people about your books. Most importantly, use it...use it...use it!

Does it work? This is an example of how branding works at its best. It is not my "Explore roads less traveled in a Janet Elaine Smith Novel," but it does prove the point. For some reason, quite some time ago people began referring to me as "JES" instead of "Janet Elaine Smith." I don't know exactly how that came about. I never sign my e-mails or anything else that way. But one day I had an e-mail from a dear friend, a fellow writer (a very popular one) who lives in Colorado. She was in a Barnes & Noble bookstore when somebody walked up to the information desk and asked the attendant, "Do you know if there is a new JES book out?"

My friend, the eavesdropper, snickered to herself, thinking that the customer might be referring to me. She said what really blew her away, though, was when the clerk immediately said, "Oh, yes! Her newest one is *Bank Roll*. Come on, I'll show you where it is."

Yes, my friends, the proof of the pudding is in the eating. Here's hoping people are swallowing every single word you write. Maybe one day we will all be as famous as Campbell's Chicken Noodle Soup. *Mmmm, mmmm good!* Yup, that's more branding!

Chapter 28
Janet Elaine Smith's Top 10 Marketing Tips

If you need a quick "refresher course" before you head out the door, here's the best of the bunch. I would suggest that you print these off and keep them handy at all times. Above all, remember to have fun! I often tell people that this is the hardest job I've ever done, but it's also sure the most fun one!

1. Be a lurker—Hang out in the section in bookstores where your books are. When someone looks for a book, offer them yours.

2. Never hide your book—At a restaurant, set it on the table; make a see-through pocket in your purse and stick your book in it.

3. If you've got it, flaunt it—wear your book cover on a sweatshirt or t-shirt; put it on a cap; make pins to wear and to give away.

4. You asked for it, you've got it—don't let Toyota do it alone. If a cashier asks for picture ID, show them your picture on the book. Let them write down the ISBN instead of your driver's license number.

5. Never hang up on a telemarketer—let them finish their pitch and then give them yours. You can sell hundreds of books this way!

6. Don't be afraid to interrupt—even on the Internet. If someone in a thread mentions something that pertains to your book, jump in with a bit of BSP (blatant self-promotion).

7. Blow your own horn—have bumper stickers made up to put on your car and to give to others. Like "Honk if you've read a Janet Elaine Smith novel."

8. Attend book signings—book in hand. If another author is signing their books, support them by buying their book; then show them your book.

9. Become a part of "bookstore mania"—call bookstores (start in your area and then venture out). Make them want to buy your book.

10. Become an eavesdropper—when you hear someone say it's their anniversary or a birthday, give them a book. They are almost certain to buy any other books you write. And they may well buy them for Christmas gifts.

A NOTE FROM THE AUTHOR

This is just the tip of the iceberg, but we all know the icebergs are melting, so don't be left running into the mainstream of promotion. Dare to be different! Use your imagination. You did that to write your book, so just extend that creativity to writing your own marketing plan.

One word of caution: in today's cyber-world, things change so rapidly that it is almost impossible to keep up with any information on the virtual highway known as the Internet. There are sure to be urls in this book, as in any other that deals with the Internet, that have changed. Don't let that discourage you. You can always go to Google (or your favorite search engine) and type in the name to see if the company or reference you are looking for has moved. If you still can't find it, do a search for the topic and you are bound to come up with a whole new list of places to find similar information. In fact, it is a good idea to do a new search for things all the time. You don't want your marketing efforts to become stagnant, so keep them fresh by staying "in the know."

Whatever you do, do it with your whole heart and soul. If you do, people will recognize your passion for your books, and that passion and enthusiasm is contagious. It can spread faster than an outbreak of salmonella from tainted spinach!

As I end each of my marketing columns in *Writers Journal,* "Happy sales to you!"

About the Author

Janet Elaine Smith came on the book scene in June 2000, with the publication of *Dunnottar*, her first novel. In less than four months, it was the No. 1 best-selling Scottish book on Amazon.com (out of over 8000 titles), a position it held for nearly three months.

Janet is now the author of sixteen published novels, and the Marketing Director for Star Publish LLC. What was her secret? She credits three things: God blessed her work, dumb beginner's luck, and just plain hard work.

Janet and her husband, Ivan, live in Grand Forks, North Dakota.